D1546364

Simply Frank

The Story Behind
the Man, the Brand and
Let Me Be Frank Productions

Frank R. Hermans and
Andrew Kruse-Ross

Foreword by Denis Gullickson

What people are saying about *Simply Frank*

"I bought a copy or maybe Frank gave me one. Either way, never read it."
— Mike Hermans (Frank's brother)

"There were no witches or vampires, very disappointed."
— Blake Hermans (Frank's son)

"Makes a great Christmas gift. I re-gifted it to an aunt
I've never met in the U.P."
— Let Me Be Frank's season ticket holder

"Every few years a book comes along that touches your soul, this isn't it."
— Andrew Kruse-Ross (co-author)

"A great read; I fell asleep after the first chapter. A wonderful sleep aid."
— Amy Riemer (Frank's wife)

"Why?"
— local pizza expert

"Frank's put a lot of himself into this book; it's complete bullshit."
— LMBF's cast member

"No, I'm serious, why?"
— local pizza expert

Reasons to purchase *Simply Frank*

It's only $10; your babysitter cost $30 for God's sake.

It's like a novel but way different.

It supports Frank's favorite charity: his pocket.

It has pictures.

It has nude pictures of Ernest Borgnine inside (just kidding).

It costs as much as the I-294 toll.
You gotta pay to get to the end, just saying.

FOREWORD
Permission to Speak Frankly ... and Simply

What an honor to be asked to write the foreword for this book.

And where to begin with these first few lines about the one and only Frank Hermans?

As a baby boomer who grew up in Green Bay, I am a fan of all things "Titletown." I come by it earnestly: I was a Westside kid knocking about this city in the sixties and seventies and I've watched and partaken in its ebb and flow from a horse farm west of town since then.

And, when it comes to Green Bay, what's not to like?

Well, winter. But, other than that, what?

Natural beauty. Friendly people. Great history and tradition. Opportunity. Recreation. Business, industry and education. A world-famous phenomenon known as the Green Bay Packers. Cheese. Beer. Roundabouts.

The list goes on and on.

And then there's the "Frank" of "Let Me Be Franks Productions."

Picture one of those one-man-band street performers and you have a pretty decent, figurative picture of Frank Hermans — his frenetic daily schedule ... his seamless balancing of a vast array of commitments ... his comings and goings from meeting upon meeting and task upon task ... his embracing of all that is "our neck of the woods."

Frank is, quite literally, one of the very hardest-working people in "show biz" in Green Bay. It's his passion, his joy, his essence.

And what keeps it all going, harmonized, syncopated and so on? How does he keep all those instruments and doodads in time and in tune?

Well, there's talent and drive and creativity and hard-damned work and perseverance and cleverness for sure. There's also warmth and compassion and openness and graciousness and a whole lot of other human qualities apparent in each of Frank's interactions — whether with an audience of several hundred or a lone audience member after a show.
There's a whole lot of love, too. Love for his family, his fellow performers,

his audience, his associates and, of course, his community.

Frank's family consists of Frank's "dream girl," Amy, and his "wonderful kids," Josh, Austin, Blake, Katrina, Harrison, Jack, Vivian and stepson Darien.

Frank's other "family" is that talented troupe of performers who take the stage with him for one of those "Let Me Be Franks Productions." As he says with actual modesty, "To be successful, you hire people who are more talented than you are!"

Each of these loves is a sweet tinkling on those dangling chimes draped over his left shoulder.

His strong, steady set of show dates at the Meyer Theatre is the bedrock of "dinner theater"-style entertainment in this town. On that note, Frank has played a huge role in revitalizing Green Bay's downtown.

Indeed, for 17 years, Frank and company have been making audiences laugh and sing-along. Add in the fact that those shows wonderfully embrace the life, verve and quirky culture that is Northeastern Wisconsin and you've got something rather unique.

And Frank's shows are unique. And delightful. Half musical revue, half comedic romp and the third half holding up a mirror to all of us. You cannot sit through one of Frank's shows without tapping your foot, joining the chorus or laughing until your belly aches and your cheeks turn a little bit red. You also can't help but leave with a smile in your heart.

Some suggest that it's all one basic, fun-loaded, musically-rich script. But the nuances are molded to fit Clintonville's underground tremors, Denmark's after-school activity bus, Duck Creek's "dynasty," Kewaunee's junk pickers, Manitowoc's pots and pans and the U.P.'s housewives.

A quick strum of the guitar and a couple of clanks on the cowbell and we're off to the next project.

And Frank isn't just a one-tune one-man band. By no means. His repertoire is extensive and it's all delivered with great dexterity.

You can catch Frank as a fill-in co-host of Local Five Live on WFRV-TV Channel 5 and see Frank and his band, "3rd and Short," on Larry McCarren's "Packers Live" on NBC-TV 26. Come March, Frank will submit his

12th year as co-host of the CP Telethon on WBAY-TV 2.

In 2016, he was named Best of the Bay musician by the Green Bay Press-Gazette for the sixth time. Frank's Musical Tribute Shows continue to grow with over 65 performances in 2016.

Once a month, Frank's monthly magazine, Frankly Green Bay, hits nearly 300 newsstands. That publication brings the best of arts, entertainment and community to area readers.

Frankly Green Bay can be found every Wednesday at 9 a.m. on Local 5 Live. It's in these video cameos that Frank "introduces you to creative people from throughout Northeastern Wisconsin." This writer enjoyed 6:47 minutes of fame, himself, in Episode 90. What a blast!

Sprinkled in for good musical measure are two websites, franklygreenbay.com and letmebefranks.com, a Facebook page, YouTube Channel, Twitter and other social media.

Oh, and there's that history thing — a recent addition — where Frank takes a humorous look at local history such as his campy representation of early-Green Bay figure, Ebenezer Childs.

There's also the impressive work of Frank's business and creative partner, Pat Hibbard, an integral part of Let Me Be Frank Productions for 14 years. Pat is Frank's business partner, co-writer, and co-director of all the "Frank Shows." Pat's own resume and schedule is an opus including involvement in the area music scene through "Music U: Student to Stage" and as bass player for several area bands.

You sometimes wonder where it all comes from, but then you realize that it all comes from the same spot — a heart of gold that loves it all.

On a personal note, thanks to Frank for his membership on the board of the Green Bay Theatre Company and his friendship and sage advice on any number of fronts. Also, thanks to Andrew Kruse-Ross, the editor of "Frankly Green Bay," the author of this book and another wildly-talented friend.

So … bang that drum, toot that horn, strum that guitar, tweet that whistle, rattle that tambourine, clang that bell, trill that kazoo, and hum that tune. Here's to Frank Hermans and all things "Frank."
And here's to the music and the laughter continuing for a long, long time.

As they say, "Get your laugh on with Frank."

And, now … Enjoy the read.

— *Denis Gullickson*

PREFACE

About four years ago, I was approached by someone interested in writing a book about the beginning and the rise of Let Me Be Frank Productions. Let's just say I was blindsided, skeptical and flattered all at the same time. To think that someone would even mention the thought? At first, I my thinking was, "Why would someone even care about LMBF's?" Then that same person told me that they wrote books about successful people for a fee. This I totally understood and I toyed with the idea for some time.

After giving it some thought, I recalled all the really good things LMBF's has done and the struggle that took place to get where we are. I remembered the pitfalls and the heartbreaks and then wondered if I wanted the public to know about these things.

I wasn't ready, so I respectfully declined. I was very tempted, but the thought of a tell-all book about us just wasn't in the cards … yet.

It was also about four years ago that I met the co-author of this book, Andrew Kruse. He was the editor of the Chilton Times-Journal and the Green Bay edition of the SCENE newspaper. Today, he's my editor and you may know him from Frankly Green Bay, the monthly magazine that we co-founded with my brother Mike Hermans.

I was somewhat skeptical if our publication would be successful, but we launched with a soft opening in February of 2015. At that time, we were printing 3,000 copies of our 32-page issue that was available at 120 or so locations. Currently, we're generally at 40 pages per issue and distributing 9,000 – 10,000 issues every month at over 280 locations. Not bad! And those numbers continue to grow.

It seems we'd created a magazine that was just what the people of Brown County wanted.

Having seen the success of Frankly Green Bay, about a year ago, I approached Andrew about the idea of writing a book about Let Me Be Frank Productions. He jumped at the chance but was concerned about time; we had 11 months to write, proof, print and be ready for Christmas.

Well, folks, we did it, or Andrew did it.

I have to say, there are many things in this book I didn't think I could really talk about, as they are somewhat emotional. We both fought to get me to open up on a few issues with LMBF history, and I feel that this is the truest account of my thoughts regarding the beginnings and the continued success of the company.

With that said, I hope you enjoy the book; it's an easy read and digs into the parts of LMBF that only a selected few know. It is my hope to write a continuation for next year, so look for that around Christmas of 2017.

Before you read on, please know that LMBF's isn't built on my shoulders alone, it's built upon the shoulders of the entire troupe. Each member brings talents to the troupe that could thrive in a bigger market, but folks stay here in Green Bay because this is home.

I've had the incredible experience of working with some of the best talent Wisconsin has to offer. Two people in particular deserve special mention: Pat Hibbard and Amy Riemer.

Pat Hibbard is my business partner and one of the smartest people I know. I'm lucky to be able to write shows with such a great guy.

My wife, Amy, showed me that happiness is something real. She is the real cog behind LMBF's and has the innate ability to keep me focused. Where I am a big picture guy, she is detail oriented. She'll tell me to look at things with my "girl eyes" when making assessments, and it works.

A big thank you needs to go to our current cast. They're amazing and make it all possible: Dennis Panneck, Tony Pilz, Adam Cain, Pat Hibbard, Jeff Arnold, Heath Hermans, Lisa Borley, Kasey Corrado (also a columnist for Frankly Green Bay), Kelly Guslof, David Guslof, Tom Verbrick, Emily Paulsen, Mike Hermans, Tracey Cook and Kelly Klaus.

Also a big thank you to all the former performers for Let Me Be Franks; without you this would not have been possible: Emily Moore, Cassidy Dittmer, Dan Rafferty, Jenny Thiel, Maggie Dame, Lee Starks, Tommy Reynolds, Adam Bunn, Darren Johnson, Shelly Lahti-Emmer, Jeni Funk, Jennifer Polera, Ben Cahall, Paul Evansen, Karen Coppersmith, Julio Reyes, Jolene Van Beek, Danny Lueck, Tamara Becker, Austin Rockstroh, Jack Janowicz, Joy Rockstroh, Linda Roach, Oscar Pilz and Joe Pilz.

I would personally like to thank the management and staff at the Meyer Theatre including Matt Goebel, for your expertise in the field and allowing us to do what we love. To Mr. Tim Funk, thanks for your demeanor and your direct approach to sound and technical issues. Mr. Dennis O'Donnell, thank you for your unbridled enthusiasm for theatre and your front house management that makes us look professional. Thanks also to the management team of PMI who hire us to do this crazy stuff and write the checks.

A few of my mentors I would like to thank who have helped bend and shape me along the way: my mother Karen Coppersmith, Mr. Ed Van Boxtel, Kramer Rock, Andy Persani, Lance Broberg, Janice Hirth and my best bud, Paul Hartford.

And the biggest thank you and kudos go to the co-author of this book; Mr. Andrew Kruse, you truly are a talent that I'm glad I have the opportunity to work with you and be your friend.

— Frank R. Hermans

ACKNOWLEDGEMENT

The authors would like to extend their gratitude and appreciation to those that assisted either directly or indirectly with the creation of this book: Ryne Roulette for his design expertise, DigiCopy for their technical assistance, Karen Coppersmith for archiving so much of Frank and the troupe's history, Warren Gerds and the Green Bay Press-Gazette for years of coverage, Aimee Suzanne Kruse-Ross for picking up so much slack over the last year, and, last but not least, all our family and friends for their continuous support and encouragement.

INTRODUCTION

Chances are, if you're reading this now, you've some idea about who Frank Hermans is — or at least you think you do. You've likely seen him hosting the news on TV 5, or maybe caught him performing as Elvis at an event, maybe he even appeared at your office one day to deliver a singing telegram, perhaps you've seen him leading 3rd and Short on Larry McCarren's show or tuned in to see him during the annual CP telethon. Maybe he's helped raise money for a charity or organization that's close to your heart or maybe he saved your life when your heart stopped, maybe you simply know him as the face of Let Me Be Frank Productions. No matter how you know Frank, this book is designed to bring you a little closer to the man himself.

If you've ever wondered how Let Me Be Frank Productions came into being, or how the troupe came to call the Meyer Theatre home, or wondered what Frank's early performances looked like or wondered what Frank might be doing if he wasn't in front of an audience, you'll likely enjoy what is to follow.

Should you read on, be prepared for a light read that covers Frank's early childhood, his aspirations and business endeavors, how he made his way to the stage and chronicles the formation of a Northeastern Wisconsin favorite: Let Me Be Frank Productions. What we've prepared for you isn't high art, and, if I've done my job properly, you should find the book to mirror a tone not too dissimilar to that of a Let Me Be Frank show. Sure, some of the topics discussed within aren't that humorous, but most are handled with a light touch. Cliché, idiom and assorted wordplay have not been omitted, and we've offered two title options to the book's headings, so if you don't like the first one, feel free to latch onto the second. To be clear, though, this isn't a tell-all tale filled with heartbreak and secrets, this is a book created with Frank's fans and Let Me Be Frank Productions' fans in mind.

In a few short pages, you'll meet Joe Kiedinger, one of Frank's closest friends and a man that was instrumental in getting the troupe off the ground. In covering the early days of the troupe, it's apparent the while Frank is a man of wonderful — albeit sometimes crazy — ideas, his judgment of others and ability to find the right people to help bring those ideas to fruition is no less profound. So was the case with Joe nearly 20 years ago when Frank put Joe in charge of bringing his crazy idea to start a dinner theatre troupe to life. So was it too (I hope) when Frank came to me with the idea of writing this book.

I couldn't help but find myself identifying with Joe while doing so. Frank is a man of many virtues, but patience isn't necessarily one of them. He wanted the first edition completed in time for Christmas of 2016 — giving us a mere 11 months to work on the book in our "spare time." With both of us having work commitments elsewhere — he admittedly was busier than I — it was going to be tough.

About those commitments: I've known no one who makes the appointments that Frank Hermans keeps. He is the busiest, hardest working individual I've ever met. I think that fact is maybe sometimes lost upon audiences when they see him so effortlessly laying it all out there during a performance, but a great deal of effort has taken place long before he steps on stage. But he's not left to do all the work himself; Frank surrounds himself with amazing people. One need look no further than his cast for evidence.

I can't help but think about the amount of trust that Frank placed in Joe when he dropped so much into his lap during the troupe's formative days. And while I think it would be presumptuous for me to say I was equally worthy of Frank's trust in assembling this book, it is a task that despite some of the humor found within, I have not taken lightly. In short, I am honored to have played a part in the creation of this first edition of "Simply Frank."

It is from that position that I've attempted to bring Let Me Be Frank Production's greatest asset, its fans, a book that I hope will be both revealing and enjoyable.

Doing so has not always been easy. Aside from the constraints of time allotted for completion, there were many other concerns with which to contend. Not least of which was Frank's aversion to vulnerability. For a man that has so much drive and determination and so effortlessly appears before the public eye, and so openly promotes his brands, Frank can be surprisingly leery of attention. Interesting for a man whose name appears both in Let Me Be Frank Productions and Frankly Green Bay. But it may surprise you to know that neither name was his idea. Don't believe me? Keep reading.

As I've mentioned, Frank originally hoped this book would cover only the history of his troupe, he somehow thought, mistakenly, that he could be omitted from it or only play a supporting role where the book was concerned. It took some convincing to get him to see that without him there was no history to speak of, and ultimately, no book to assemble. Joe Kiedinger, when I first told him of our plans to write a book about Frank and the history of Let Me Be Frank Productions replied, "How the hell are you going to do that? Frank is one of the most intensely private individuals I know."

It wasn't easy, but I think we managed.

— *Andrew Kruse-Ross*

CONTENTS

ACT I

The Long Way Home

A BEAVER IS BORN OR
A FAMILY IN TRANSIT

Frank R. Hermans was born on July 24, 1964. He was the first of three children born to Frank Hermans Sr. and Karen Costello. Up to that time, the newlywed couple were living in a trailer parked alongside a gas station owned by a relative on Green Bay's east side in the area now occupied by the University of Wisconsin-Green Bay.

After Frank's birth, Karen refused to return to life in a trailer and the couple went straight from the hospital to living with Karen's parents. They stayed there briefly before finding a home to rent near the corner of East Mason and Main Streets. Ten months later, the couple's second child, Michael, was born.

Life for the young family wasn't easy and the family struggled financially. So tight was the family's situation that Mr. Hermans couldn't make the payments on the engagement ring he'd given his wife and Karen was forced to return the ring to the store. The couple's relationship was a rocky one. They would quarrel and reconcile, quarrel and reconcile. Reconciliation often meant a change in scenery for the family. Perhaps thinking a new setting would mean a fresh start for his family, the family uprooted itself for the first time.

"Whenever we'd get back together, [Frank Sr.] would want us to move," recalls Karen. "So we did."

The family landed in Davie, Florida, just east of Fort Lauderdale. The location was near enough to a nuclear plant where Mr. Hermans found work. Frank and Mike, who would have been 3 and 2, respectively at that time, recall little from the family's stint in Florida, except for the bugs.

"That's all I remember is a shit ton of bugs," says Mike. "Crawling on the woodwork, crawling in the tub; they were everywhere."

The family returned to Wisconsin briefly and the couple's third child, Heath, was born in the winter of '69. It wouldn't be long before the family set off again — this time across Lake Michigan to the area of Mears, Michigan.

The family settled in rural Silver Lake, Mich., in equally rural Golden Township, population 1,742 as of 2010.

Karen recalls her family's time in Michigan as being the best they ever had. Mr. Hermans found work as an electrician at Ludington's nuclear plant and the boys received their first guitars and began taking lessons. But Karen also recalls, quite vividly, young Frank's many health problems.

Both Frank and Mike suffered from allergies at an early age, but Frank, an asthmatic, wound up in the hospital with asthmatic pneumonia several times as a preschooler.

Later, as an elementary student, Frank complained of terrible stomach pains that left him nearly immobile.

"He'd be doubled over with pain," recalls his mother. "He couldn't straighten out his legs or even go to the bathroom."

Karen took Frank to see a doctor. The culprit: gas. Well, sort of.

"I remember drinking Coke as a child," recalls Frank, "because it would make me burp and relieve some of the pain."

During an episode in class at church, Frank's teachers called Karen at home. His mother picked him up and rushed him back to the doctor's. At the doctor's office, Frank was hooked into an encephalograph to check for unusual brain activity. The scan revealed an unusual waveform. Frank's brain was sending a signal to his bowels causing convulsions that mimicked the acute pain or cramping caused by excessive gas.

He was given a strong medication that had to be graduated to the proper dosage. The regiment was maintained for about a year, but affected his personality. After a year, Karen began to wean him off of his meds. The problem never returned.

It's also as an elementary student that Frank fell in love with television commercials for Ipana toothpaste featuring Bucky Beaver — the animated beaver brought to life by Disney animator David Hilberman and voiced by Mouseketeer Jimmie Dodd.

Frank was hooked on Bucky and his "Brusha, brusha, brusha" jingle.

"When that beaver would come on, he'd press his face up against that television. He loved that beaver, loved him!" says Karen.

To this day, close family members, including his mother, call Frank by his nickname, Beaver.

The family's stay in Michigan didn't last, and again they found themselves heading south, settling for a brief but memorable year in Arkansas.

Karen doesn't hide her displeasure in the family's stay in Huff, Arkansas. Although admittedly beautiful, the area left little for her and her boys — Frank and Mike were now in high school — to do (apart from partaking in chewing tobacco, apparently). If Silver Lake had been rural, Huff couldn't have been more than a stone's throw from the fictional Cahulawassee River in "Deliverance."

In 2000, Pleasant Plains, the town where the boys went to school, reported a population of 267.

"The first six months there were terrible," recalls Frank. "I hated it. Lots of loneliness."

Arkansas wasn't completely full of strangers, however, Frank's aunt Barb and uncle Butch lived nearby. It was in the couple's basement, listening to records that Frank and Mike got their first vocal lessons. One album in particular, a double-LP, mail-order recording by Elvis Presley simply titled "Elvis" captivated the boys.

"Oh, we'd play that record in my aunt's basement over and over, singing along and staring at the cover," says Frank.

Today, that very copy of "Elvis" resides in Mike's record collection.

Much of the move to Arkansas left the boys in culture shock. At school, classes were small and punishments harsh — often involving a paddle.

"Oh, that school was a piece of crap," recalls Karen, "not a place you'd want your daughters to attend, that's for sure."

Halfway through his sophomore school year, Frank began to enjoy his new school and began to stand out among his classmates. He played on his school's basketball team and even began to excel academically — albeit with a little deviancy.

He went all the way to the state level with a science fair presentation, claiming he'd grown a paramecium specimen in a petri dish at home. He hadn't. And most of the information he reported as his own was, in fact, pulled from textbooks, but no one was the wiser. This was the first instance that Frank recognized a penchant for being able to "bullshit" his way through life's obstacles.

With no one calling his research into question, and with only 32 other students in his sophomore class, Frank would have been a likely valedictorian candidate. Regardless of his methods, it was as a sophomore in a small Arkansas classroom that Frank began to enjoy school.

But whatever the area lacked in cutting edge educational practices it made up for in beautiful expanses, which was a good thing considering only one channel came in on the family television. The Hermans' property sat among thousands of acres owned by their nearest neighbor, Mr. Bryant, and the boys took to the country life, hunting, spending much time exploring the slopes of the area's many named mountains and cooling off in Salado Creek.

Frank and Mike walked into the world of "Mutual of Omaha's Wild Kingdom" whenever they stepped outside, and they did so often. Their father encouraged hunting and the boys obliged, and frequently set off into the woods with a 20-gauge and a box of shells.

"I would bring home squirrels, I would bring home rabbits," says Frank. "Mom says we never ate those things, but we did."

When not hunting game with a shotgun, the boys would fashion spears by attaching knives to long sticks with which to hunt snakes for fun. King snakes, copperheads and water moccasins all fell victim to the Hermans boys. Once dispatched, Frank recalls removing the heads of their quarry so that their venom could be more easily extracted.

On less fruitful days, when boredom would set in, activities included culling members from the brood of chickens — many of them infected with bumblefoot — that had the run of the Hermans' yard or enjoying the extra curricular benefits of F.F.A. membership. The latter usually left them a mess.

"I had a pig for F.F.A.," tells Mike. "We used to steal bread bags from my mom and dad and fill 'em with pig shit and chuck 'em at semi trucks! Man, did we stink!"

Whether it did much to rid the Hermans boys of their odor, area children made swimming trips in Salado Creek regularly, but the country life wasn't without its dangers. A fishing trip on Salado Creek claimed the lives of two of their classmates, and Frank recalls pulling a friend from the creek after a flood, doing so nearly cost him his own life.

Perhaps most significant during this time was Frank's first love. Her name was Lacretia and Frank had fallen for her deeply. When it was announced the family would again be moving, Frank was heartbroken.

Upon hearing the news, Frank confined himself to his bed where he would stare at the ceiling for hours on end.

"Oh, I thought Beaver was going to do something drastic," says his mother.

Frank left his classmates in Arkansas after only a year. In his only yearbook from that experience Frank was named class clown, class egotist, class big mouth and together with Lucretia, best couple — at least that's how he remembers it.

Eventually, the family found its way back to Green Bay, where the boys would attend Preble High School. The constant moves made life, especially life at school, difficult for the boys. Their lifestyle didn't leave them much time to make friends, so they looked to each other for support.

At Preble, Frank is able to get comfortable. He's a good student. He participates in theatre and his musical ability makes him a popular kid.

Things weren't so for Mike, who's had enough of being the new kid at an endless change of schools. He's always been the family's independent thinker. Conformity isn't his strong suit.

"My Michael always had to do things the hard way," says Karen. "You'd tell him what to do and he'd listen — he was never disrespectful, none of the boys were — but then he'd go out that door and do just the opposite."

Mike was the family's black sheep. Where the rest of his family is quite vocal about their aversion to life in rural Arkansas, Mike feels quite the opposite and admits something about the freedom he experienced there left him enthralled. A few weeks into his junior year, Mike dropped out of school. He wouldn't be sitting still for long, though. In fact, he immediately begins preparing for his GED — which he received before his former classmates received their diplomas.

By this time, a teenage Frank has stepped up to help his mother as much as possible. He takes on the role of helper to his working mother and protector to his brothers, especially Heath.

"He was always my helper," recalls Karen. "He became like Heath's surrogate father."

As a helper, if Frank couldn't persuade his brothers to help with the chores, he'd end up doing them himself. He recalls his father would come home from work and place his hand on the television to see if it was warm. A warm television and unfinished chores meant trouble for the boys.

Of course, the role of protector was only fulfilled when he and Mike weren't attacking each other, as happened on a few occasions.

While the boys were living in Denmark, Wis., Frank recalls being unable to convince Mike to help with chores. As Mike defiantly played outside with the family's horse, Sundance, Frank's anger grew until it hit a boiling point.

He crept to an open window, bb gun in hand and waited for the opportunity to exact his revenge. The shot hit Mike in the back of the leg. Perhaps thinking Mike might think an angry wasp was the source of the pain, Frank slowly retreated from his firing position, but not before Mike caught a glimpse of the barrel being slowly pulled back through the window.

Another occasion, naturally, involved a girl. Kelly Smith was her name. Mike recalls her being one of his closest friends. Eventually Mike realized his feelings for her went beyond mere friendship. That changed when he walked into the house one day to find Kelly and Frank locked in an embrace in dad's armchair. Mike managed to maintain his rage and left the couple as he found them.

"Man, I was so pissed I just left the house for a while," recalls Mike.

Perhaps thinking the walk would cool him off, Mike walked aimlessly about the neighborhood, but eventually returned home where he greeted Frank's jaw with his fist. The two scuffled. In the fracas Mike took a blow that knocked him back and into the family's antique desk, snapping a table leg.

The unforeseen collateral damage brought all hostilities to an abrupt and unconditional end. The two joined forces and set to work to repair the damage before their parents came home from work. The alliance was a success and it was years before their parents would discover anything had happened to their prized piece of furniture.

In 1980 Frank Sr. and Karen call it quits for good and the couple divorce. The boys cope as they always had, by leaning on each other. This time, they form their first band. They call themselves Facked.

—*A Message from Frank* —

In the beginning I loved moving, new place, new girls. It was exciting! And it seemed we would always come back to Denmark or Green Bay after a year or so. I believe the moving around made us boys more gregarious than most others, we had to make friends. I still recall the groups at some schools; Gear Heads, Farmers, Jocks, Dopers. Well, I was friends with all of them because I had no history with anyone. I did meet my best friend Paul Hartford my junior year at Preble. We were both the new kid, he was from Premontre and I was from Arkansas, quite the combo. I was happy that my parents divorced, it made me a nervous wreck to hear the fighting all the time and I had a constant fear of my father. Sometimes I think I really never knew what a stable household was and maybe that has shown in my own personal decisions and relationships.

My brothers, Heath and Mike, are my best friends, we moved all over the country together, bonded over our parents' divorce and had that Hermans' confidence. We enjoyed many of the same things: humor, music, drinking. We have been in bands together since we were teenagers, with Heath being only 14 on our first paying gig. We've remained close throughout thick and thin, through ex-wives and through failed businesses. I wish every family had what we have. Sure we fight, but we also forgive and move on. If we couldn't have done that I think it would have been a tragedy.

PIZZA HEAT AND SWISS SEATS OR SHOW ME THE HARD WAY HOME

Shortly after graduation from high school in '82, Frank and Mike moved out of their dad's house and ventured off on their own.

For $135 a month the boys rented a shack on Velp Ave. Basically, a converted vacation cabin, the shack was cramped, — no larger than the most basic studio apartment — rat infested and cold.

Unable to afford the gas bill, the boys utilized a countertop pizza oven for heat. The device was less than efficient.

"You'd go to bed cold, wake up in the middle of the night sweating, shut off the glowing oven and wake up in the morning freezing," recalls Mike.

Frank attended UWGB from '82 – '86 and as Mike recalls, most of his student loan money went to buy equipment for a succession of bands and musical endeavors. When not performing live music, Frank was living the good life making six bucks an hour as a DJ at the local Doc & Eddy's.

"It was more money than I knew what to do with," says Frank.

Frank must have impressed some in management and was offered an assistant manager position with the bar. He took it and all went well until one day, someone from corporate came through the door — someone Frank had never met — and said Doc's was closing its doors for good.

Unbeknownst to Frank, there had been a lot of changes in the company's upper echelon and that spelled trouble for the franchises in Wisconsin. All three Wisconsin franchises got the axe.

As compensation of sorts, Frank was offered to take up his current position with a Doc & Eddy's location in Columbia, Missouri. He accepted, married his then-girlfriend, Michelle, and settled in the Show Me state.

Frank's time behind Doc's bar took on a sort of life of its own, resulting in both positive and negative ways. It's here, in the shadow of the University of Missouri that Frank first began to shine as an entertainment promoter. Left in charge of marketing the events he'd book, Frank took to the local airwaves to promote.

"I started booking stuff for the bar and doing commercials on the radio. Comedians, bands, Chippendales, lingerie parties, I booked everything to make it a party at Doc's, and it was," says Frank.

It's also here that Frank perused new hobbies like spelunking and rock climbing. How he approached these hobbies is somewhat reflective of how he lived his life. In those days, the thought of death never entered his mind as he and his friends didn't think twice to repel down rock faces, sometimes 200-feet high, in Swiss Seats they'd tied themselves of half-inch rope. He still bears a scar from one of those early outings. It was as a rock climber that Frank earned his second nickname, Hard Way Hermans. The moniker stuck and Doc's even named a sandwich after him. Ordering the Hard Way Special at Doc & Eddy's got you a turkey cheddar melt on a croissant with your choice of side and a drink for $3.

His career life wasn't much different. Frank had Doc's rocking, but in doing so, he'd placed himself at the center of a seemingly endless party. A Monday night at a college town bar looked an awful lot like a Saturday night and that simply didn't agree with family life.

"There's no way around it, I just wasn't ready to be married," admits Frank.

For whatever reason, Frank has always identified as a Wisconsinite, more specifically, a northeastern Wisconsinite. Despite spending time growing up in Florida, Arkansas and Michigan, it was his family's stint in Denmark and Green Bay that he most enjoyed and he longed for an opportunity to return to what he considers "home."

"I really missed home. I used to have the Green Bay Press-Gazette mailed to me and I'd scour through it looking for jobs."

One of Frank's mentors, Larry Reich, left Doc & Eddy's to work for bowling giant Gala Lanes in Chicago. Having seen the success of Doc & Eddy's, which was an early example of the emerging sports bar craze, Gala had decided to get in on the action and was opening a series of sports bars inside their large bowling facilities and they needed a manager.

It wasn't quite Green Bay, but it was certainly closer to home and it came with a considerable pay increase. Frank was offered a salary of $25,000 to move to Chicago, a 38 percent increase from what he was earning at Doc & Eddy's. He moved his family to Naperville, a suburb of Chicago and began managing the new MVP Sports Bar in Carol Stream, Ill.

Here Frank employed the same tricks that had made Doc's a success and a few new ones. The venue had previously been a disco, and Frank readily took to using the equipment to DJ at the new venue. MVP Sports sat right in the heart of a rabid Blackhawk community, and with many games going untelevized in the area, Frank mastered the use of 1988 satellite television to bring the games to his clientele. That year presented a Cinderella season of sorts for the Chicago Blackhawks. Coach Mike Keenan, in his first year behind the Chicago bench, led the team, which featured an 18-year-old rookie named Jeremy Roenick, to the playoffs. Despite having the worst record of any playoff team that season, they beat the first place Detroit Red Wings and the higher seeded St. Louis Blues before advancing to the Campbell Conference Finals, where they lost to eventual Stanley Cup champs, the Calgary Flames in five games.

"It was crazy how these fans were," remembers Frank. "I'd have 400 people in that bar just to watch the Blackhawks play. It was nuts."

Another crowd pleaser, and representative of some of Frank's new tricks, was the three-foot hotdog, which was the brainchild of both Frank and Larry. When ordered, the ten-dollar yard of tubed meat was brought to the table on a stretcher to the blaring sound of sirens.

MVP kept Frank busy. He regularly spent 80 hours a week at the bar, but he managed to continue performing in bands. One in particular, called Menagerie, which featured Frank Hermans as its lead singer, made a name for itself on the local scene, even opening for a touring Skid Row at Chicago's Thirsty Whale. The band cut a demo of songs Frank had penned the lyrics to in the same studio where Survivor had laid down their tracks. While recording with Menagerie, Frank got an inclining of his vocal limitations, ones which would pop up again in the future.

"They asked me to harmonize with myself and I was like 'What the hell is that?'"

Frank could wail. A Menagerie set often included covers of hair metal groups like Cinderella, but his voice training came from singing along to records. Harmonies, sight-reading? Who needed it? Not him. Not yet.

Just as Frank had enjoyed his time at Doc & Eddy's so was it true with MVP, but he still longed to be back in Wisconsin. In 1989, he applied for a position as a beverage director for Fox Hills Resort in Mishicot, Wis. He landed an interview and was hired on the spot. Frank moved his wife and newborn son, Josh, to Two Rivers.

"I was committed to doing something different, trying to be a good dad and a good husband, but it never happened."

If Frank was looking for a change in scenery where his career was concerned, Fox Hills Resort was a poor choice. Just as with Doc's and MVP, Fox Hills was a local party hotspot and he was soon engulfed in his work.

When the Fox Hills house band left, Frank stepped up to offer his services and began landing entertainment for the venue. Comedy, strippers and bands were the order of the day.

As far as musical tastes went, the crowd at Fox Hills differed from that of Chicago and Frank selected acts he felt best suited his clientele. Hair metal wasn't going to fly. It's during this time that Frank began making connections with some of Wisconsin's best talent, forging relationships with acts like Royal Purple and Vic Ferrari.

Any deficiency in Frank's hair metal quotient he made up for with his new band Heaven Sent. Reviving many of the songs he performed with Menagerie, including covers by White Lion, Mötley Crüe and others, the band would land $200 a night.

Still 37 miles from Green Bay, Frank didn't feel he had made it home and always kept an eye on the job market for openings that would get him back to Green Bay. When he saw an opening for a beverage manager at Purcell's, located inside Green Bay's Radisson, he had to apply.

Frank recalls his endorsements from previous employers as a mixed bag. He recalls them thusly:

"Great people person, just not detail oriented."
"Has great ideas, but lacks follow-through."

Whatever they were looking for, they must have figured Frank could deliver; he was offered the job and accepted. Frank was coming home.

— *A Message from Frank* —

College was a blast for me. I was never a great student (failed a whole semester once with WF's, withdrawal fails). A GPA of 2.0 was just OK with me. Since then, I continue to take online courses thru UWGB in history and political science, I just love this stuff. Hence why one of my favorite things to do is my video series "The History Bluff." When my wife and I travel, I love to shoot at historical places and make stuff up and she corrects me … kind of like real life.

ACT II

Let's Party Like It's 1999

COLD CALL THAT CENTER OR
COME FOLLOW THE BANDS

The year was 1990 and Frank was working as the beverage manager at Purcell's, located inside the Green Bay's Radisson Hotel. At the time, a motivated Frank Hermans was looking to set his bar ahead of the competition, not for monetary gain, but for the glory.

"I didn't care about the money," recalls Frank. "My motivations have always been about the fun, the adventure. I was just always thinking about how to make that place rocking — make it kick ass."

Frank's had picked up a number of tricks during his years behind various bars. During his days in Chicago, Frank experienced karaoke in action for the first time. So impressed was he that he purchased a karaoke system for Purcell's — possibly Green Bay's first — for a sum of $10,000. Purcell's patrons loved it.

Complacency wasn't in Frank's game plan; he was always looking for new ways to make an already happening club climb to the next level. When he caught word that the popular nightclub The Top Shelf was dropping their live music nights in favor of disc jockeys, Frank saw an opportunity to have Purcell's step up its game. He promptly picked up the phone.

"I called up the agents that handled booking those bands and I got them to play at my place instead. Just like that, I've got the best live bands in the state."

The move paid off in more ways than one, as Frank would form lasting relationships with some of the best musicians in the state. One of those relationships involved current LMBF bandleader and Music U co-founder, Dennis Panneck, who, in those days, was a member of band Juke Box Heroes.

Word was spreading quickly that Purcell's was *the* place for live music, but anyone that didn't hear that from friends likely heard it over the airwaves. Frank's Frankman radio campaigns are a thing of local legend. Had the internet been in 2000 what it is today, Frank's radio campaigns may have been considered "viral" in popularity. So popular were Frank's radio commercials as The Frankman — a character inspired by Rob Schneider's Saturday Night Live character The Richemeister — that the radio station even held contests to see which callers could mimic The Frankman the closest.

"It's crazy," says Hermans, "but I still have people come up to me and say 'Hola, this is the Frankman!' which was how I started all those commercials."

Purcell's was indeed a hit, only Ashwaubenon Bowling Alley sold more beer in Green Bay in the early '90s.

"We we're always neck and neck with them in beer sales. But that was a different time. People still came to happy hour, that's what you did after work."

Purcell's was a hit, but Frank wasn't one to sit still and bask in the success. He was already looking for what was next. With his bar already rocking, Frank would have to pull out all the stops in order to take his bar to the next level; he did so by making a play to bring "Larry McCarren's Locker Room" to Purcell's.

Rumor had it that McCarren wasn't content with his filming location and might be seeking out a new venue in which to record his program.

In an action that could be considered many things: fearless, stupid, bold, reckless, Frank acted upon the rumor and began to place phone calls to McCarren's people.

Frank had no real connection to McCarren or his show, so he'd have to start from square one if he were to entice the Packer Hall of Famer to move to Purcell's, but somehow, Frank felt he had enough history with Larry to set any fears aside.

"He visited my school when I was in sixth grade," says Frank. "I don't know, somehow that seemed like I knew the guy. I didn't, but that seemed like enough to give it a shot."

I can't remember who I called or who I talked to, but I got ahold of somebody and said, "Hey, I got a place for Larry McCarren if you guys are unhappy there."

Frank was able to generate enough interest that McCarren and his people came out to Purcell's to size up the place. The timing was perfect. Purcell's was busy with renovations at the time, which allowed changes to accommodate McCarren's show could more readily be made to suit the show's needs. McCarren agreed to move his program to Purcell's, and, as part of that deal, Frank agreed to assemble a new band to support the show.

Putting a band together would be a cakewalk for Frank. At that time, Frank was in a band that combined two of his loves: music and comedy. The Rude Boys as they were called, consisted of Frank Hermans on vocals and rhythm guitar, Larry Monohan on guitar, Lee Starks on bass and Brad Miller on drums. The Rude Boys lived up to their name. A Rude Boys show might include any of a number of comedy routines laced in between a setlist (made up mostly of '70s rock tunes). During a show, the audience might witness the firing of the band's drummer for failing to learn the songs or the band might walk off stage and refuse to play if the audience didn't start buying them shots. The whole show was an act and one that audiences seemed to enjoy — the band created enough buzz that a young Pat Hibbard came to check them out, more on him later.

With a name change and omission of the comedy routine, the first incarnation of 3ʳᵈ and Short was born. McCarren had his house band.

Both Monohan and Miller's time with the band was short-lived. The former left the group angrily after an audience member's coaster connected with his head during a set. Monohan was replaced by guitarist Tom Reynolds, while the youngest of the Hermans boys, Heath, took up duties behind the kit. Despite changes to its personnel over the years, 3ʳᵈ and Short remains McCarren's official band to this very day. Throughout its history, 3ʳᵈ and Short has mirrored the Frank's Dinner Theatre and Let Me Be Frank bands. Today, 3ʳᵈ and short consists of three of the four Let Me Be Frank Band members: Dennis Panneck (guitar), Pat Hibbard (bass) and Adam Cain (drums).

Things were looking good for Purcell's and for Frank, and that's how things remained until 1994 when Frank was tempted by an offer from Ed Van Boxtel or Van Boxtel Ford.

Van Boxtel and his wife were regulars at Purcell's, often ordering pan-fried walleye on Friday nights and urging Hermans to perform Paul Anka's "Diana" on the karaoke machine. Hermans recalls him fondly as a great lover of the arts, an early mentor and a supporter of both Frank's Dinner Theatre and Let Me Be Frank Productions up until his death in 2011.

"Ed told me in that great voice of his that I could really make some money at Van Boxtel Ford."

Hermans was reluctant to take Van Boxtel up on the offer, but with a wedding on the horizon, and with assurances from Van Boxtel that he could make $50,000 a year, he accepted. Never one to burn bridges unnecessarily,

Frank continued working for Purcell's for four years, but as a consultant, handling bands and entertainment for the venue part-time. Hermans excelled at his new position, and used his acting abilities when haggling to move cars off the lot. He was especially successful at selling "old cars" (those vehicles that had been on that lot more than 60 days). Keying in on selling "old cars" came with the added bonus of extra commission for each vehicle sold. So proficient in selling was Hermans that he was awarded sales honors from Van Boxtel paid in the form of company vacations to Las Vegas. He would receive such honors three consecutive years while employed at the dealership. But by 1998 Hermans felt the moniker of car salesman was starting to stick and he was uncomfortable with that. "I just didn't want to be a car salesman the rest of my life," says Hermans. "I didn't like the stigma that people thought I was screwing them over, especially my family."

Looking for something different, Hermans responded to an ad placed by WFRV-TV 5. The station was looking for an advertising salesman. "I took the leap. I had friends that were doing well in ad sales," says Hermans.

One of those friends was 24-year-old Joe Kiedinger who was working as a salesman for WBAY. A steadfast friend, Kiedinger would become one of the founding members of Frank's Dinner Theatre — the precursor to Let Me Be Frank Productions.

Things were going well for Frank at Channel 5. He made good money and bought some toys — a boat and jet skis. Frank, in his mind, was doing the responsible thing, the adult thing. But the money didn't replace the fun he had had behind the bar at Purcell's. It wouldn't be long until he'd find himself missing the bar business in earnest.

— A Message from Frank —

It was Mr. Ed Van Boxtel who taught me to ask for the sale. I believe this has helped me throughout my adult life and career, to be not afraid to ask for the sale. This was so new to me when I started selling cars but as confidence grew and my knowledge of the Ford products grew so did my pocket book. To this day, it was the most money I have ever made, and I ask for the sale in everything I do to this day. I'm not afraid of NO, it just makes the sale better. Thank you, Ed Van Boxtel; you will always have a special place in my heart.

MEANWHILE IN OTHER PARTS OF THE CITY OR TOO MANY IRONS IN THE FIRE

Hindsight is 20/20. It should have come as no surprise to Frank just how much he'd miss the bar business once he stepped away from it. It was very much his life. While logging 70 hours a week at Purcell's, Frank wasn't satisfied. He wanted more. Somehow, and simultaneously, Frank opened two bars with his brothers, Heath and Mike, and his father, Frank Sr. Together they gave Hermans Post and Doc's Comedy Club to the greater public.

"It was a few years of extreme chaos and carousing and craziness. It was a time when we made a lot of money and we didn't save a penny because we we're young and stupid," says Frank.

Always in bands of some sort, the Hermans boys had rented out an empty space in the office building of Melotte Meats for $200 a month. Here in the appointed "party space," the boys could let their hair down and rehearse with their band Facked.

In the front of the office building was a vacant space that had once been a bar. Frank describes it as little more than a black box, but they inquired and were told they could have the space for $500 a month. They agreed and set about re-opening the space as bar — their bar. It was a logical progression in some respects, or at least it seemed so at the time. They were already renting a space in the same building to rehearse; Hermans Post, as they decided to name it, would give the band a place to perform in front of a crowd. And, by Frank's admission, a good number of brews went down while rehearsing, why not open a bar and maybe make a buck selling some of those brews?

They scrounged up some cash and opened Hermans Post on a $900 budget. A third of that money went to purchase a liquor license, another third was set aside to purchase what looked liked a used meat cooler from a neighborhood bar, and the last third was used to stock the shelves. Other equipment was picked up at auctions; most of it was given to them for nothing. The bar's décor was also done on a budget and featured painted hand, foot and even ass prints (not sure how) on the walls and ceiling. The bar proper was painted to mimic Eddie Van Halen's striped Frankenstrat guitar.

Hermans Post also featured the area's first Velcro wall. The wall was just as it sounds: a wall of Velcro. It enabled people, wearing a modified one-piece suit, to spring themselves from a trampoline against the wall and stick there. Frank had the idea while working at Purcell's. Mike designed it and their mother, Karen, sewed the Velcro suit together.

The wall was meant as an amusement, but also served a more practical purpose. "We used to have a few patrons that were paraplegics and their friends would take them out of the wheelchair and stick them on the wall so they could have a drink while standing up," recalls Frank.

With Heath operating the bar, a Velcro wall and the band Facked ready to provide patrons with entertainment, Hermans Post was ready to open its doors in 1991. It just needed a proper sign. Mike took charge of the job and chose a large pig as the bar's logo — Frank claims he has no idea why, but Mike insists the bar's mascot selection was a no-brainer.

"That's the only animal I could draw worth a shit," says Mike, who also insists it wasn't a pig he was drawing, but a razorback, in homage to his days in Arkansas.

The Hermans clan's second combined business venture took place in 1992 when they leased a space on Washington Street for $1,000 a month that was formerly known as Club Chaos. The club had a less-than-favorable reputation as hangout for underage drinkers, but Frank and company had other plans for the venue. They planned to open Green Bay's first dedicated stand-up comedy venue and they named it Doc's Comedy Club. The name was an homage to the Missouri bar where Frank first learned the business in the '80s, Doc & Eddy's.

Frank's role at Purcell's had put him in contact not only with the state's most sought after bands, but also its comedians. Comedy had done so well at Purcell's, that opening a comedy club seemed like an obvious choice.

Frank explains, "I would have Pat McCurdy come into Purcell's on a Sunday night, charge $5 at the door and that would go to Pat, netting him up to $1,200 for a Sunday night's performance. Then I'd have him headline Doc's the next night."

This system let traveling comedians make the most of their visit to Green Bay by working multiple nights. For a mere $26, Frank would put the talent up at what is now the Village Inn Motel. The occurrences at the hotel involving traveling comedians and after hour parties have become a thing of local legend, and at Frank's request, those stories won't be appearing within this book. Perhaps the follow up?

This system also worked for everyone else involved. Purcell's got their piece, Doc's got theirs and Frank got his. Was it double dipping? Yup.

"I was double dipping with everything," admits Frank, "but Purcell's was okay with it because they were so packed and so busy all the time."

Frank and family sunk $5,000 into the venue and opened the club's doors Wednesday through Saturday. The bill usually included a headliner, a feature performer and Frank serving as master of ceremonies. Many an up-and-coming comic graced Doc's stage. Among them were the likes of Jimmy Pardo and Nick DiPaolo — the latter was the venue's first headliner.

DiPaolo even lent a hand in the club's design. "Our comedy club? It looked like a shithole, I have to say it," says Frank. "But it had potential."

Frank Sr. and Mike set about customizing a bar given to them by Los Banditos East, and DiPaolo suggested moving the venue's stage to an interior wall, setting things up side-stage and blackening out the windows to add an air of mystery to the club. Frank built on the success of The Frankman radio commercials he had run for Purcell's and took Doc's Comedy Club to the airwaves. It all worked. For two years, Doc's was a success and continued to draw comedians from across the country, even seasoned acts such as Henny Youngman, checked out Doc's.

"We had so much fun," recalls Frank. "We didn't know what we had back then. When I think back to that time, we should have been millionaires, but we just pissed it all away. All of us did."

Doc's paid its headliners $500 a week, while features received $300 a week. To cover expenses, or "cover the nut," as Frank likes to say, Doc's needed 80 paying customers a night. It met those numbers readily … for a while.

Washington Street was becoming fertile ground in those days. The street was just beginning to show the early signs of blooming into what it is today, and Doc's was on prime real estate. Green Bay club owner and entrepreneur Pat Quinn, had his eye on the property and had made a tempting offer. Meanwhile, another comedy club, the Funny Bone, opened up in what is now known as the Bayside Marketplace. The rival venue flooded the market with free tickets to lure in customers, enough so that Doc's was no longer bringing in its target of 80 paid customers a night. No longer "covering the nut," and with an offer on the table from Quinn, Doc's Comedy Club was no more. Well, sort of.

Just a short walk down the street, in a building that sits atop what is now Stir-Ups Parlor & Saloon, the Hermans boys resettled. The location was a former dance studio and sported wall-to-wall mirrors. It was here the Hermans group reopened their comedy club, this time calling it Doc's Laff Factory, but the location struggled to gain the traction they had enjoyed at Doc's Comedy Club, prompting a series of format changes — none of them stuck.

The club first morphed into Green Bay's first rave club, complete with techno DJs, and later it became an after hours club, serving patrons from 2 a.m. to 6 a.m. The venue charged a $3 cover at the door, but the cost was waived for bringing in a non-perishable food item. Pizza, nachos and sodas were on the menu, but Frank isn't sure the venue was ever licensed to be selling food. One thing is certain, no health inspector ever visited during the venue's open hours. Food wasn't the only thing visitors were enjoying. Frank recalls finding evidence his patrons were sneaking in alcohol, as well as other libations.

In '96, after little more than a year, Doc's Laff Factory, in all its incarnations, closed.

"Business and family just don't mix," says Frank. "It was fun, but I think it would of torn us apart had we stayed in business."

Frank and company had been in it for the fun, and fun is easier to obtain in business when you're covering your costs. Once concerns begin to arise about who has contributed what, and prices placed upon those contributions, the venture ceases to be fun. Luckily, according to Frank, they called it quits before such concerns became an issue.

"It was just getting to be too much," recalls Frank. "I was married. My second son was born around this time. It was the right time to hang it up."

On positive notes, the venue had collected some 2,000 canned goods during the year, which were donated to a local food pantry upon the venue's closing. "We just never had time to donate them while we were open," says Frank. The comedy club experience also allowed Frank to spend more time on stage. Serving as the MC for many of the comedy shows left Frank with a 15-minute comedy routine that in his words, "sucked, but people seemed to like it."

—*A Message from Frank* —
We always went into anything we did without a plan; we had an idea but

never a plan. Mike, Heath and I would just know it would work (We called it Hermans confidence), no matter what. I had the experience and was usually the money guy, Mike was the Jack of All Trades and could build anything and Heath was a great people person, it just worked. Who can say they opened a bar with $900? Somehow we did. And the ass cheek marks on the ceiling were from my cousin Loren by the way. He got on the ladder and pressed his cheeks (with paint on them) all over the ceiling, it was amazing. You ask how did we get along so well being in that environment? Living all over the country as youths, we brothers had a bond that a little squabble couldn't ruin. We always knew when we were wrong, and didn't have a problem apologizing. Even if liquor was involved we would wait till the next day.

THE SPORTS CORNER OR BACK IN THE SADDLE

The end of 1998 and early months 1999 left Frank to do a bit of soul searching. He had discovered that despite the financial gains of selling cars, the idea of being a car salesman the rest of his life left him unfulfilled — even leaving him jaundiced at times. He had moved on and was selling advertising for TV 5, with good results, but despite the financial gains, he felt something was missing.

"I remember asking myself, 'What am I supposed to do? I'm supposed to be a dad? A husband? And have a real career, and not do all these other things?'"

In the end, Frank came to the realization that he "didn't have training to do anything else, but be an entertainer, or run something that entertained people."

He began thinking about an exit strategy that would get him back into the bar industry he so missed. One presented itself in the form of a phone call from a friend with a business opportunity. Frank's friend Casey Ladowski was entering into a partnership with several others to re-open the Sport's Corner in De Pere. They were looking for someone with experience to help run the place and offered Frank a stake in the business. Recognizing this may be the answer he was searching for, Frank signed a promissory note to the tune of $20,000 dollars and was brought in as a 25 percent owner of Sports Corner.

Early on, Frank spent his days working at TV 5 and his nights working the Sports Corner bar. Three of his partners had already committed to working fulltime to meet the demand, and Frank was eager to do the same and go all-in, but there was some hesitancy. Around six months into working the bar part-time, Frank had yet to be paid for his services. He approached his partners about it, all of whom worked the bar full-time, and, as Frank saw it, must be paying themselves something for their trouble. Frank recalls that conversation thusly:

"I see you guys all working here and I'm not getting anything…"

"Oh, you want to want to work here?"

"I've been working here."

The conversation should have been a warning sign for things to come, but such was Frank's desire to be back in the bar industry, he shrugged the situation off as an oversight.

"This was my first inclination that this probably wasn't the smartest thing I ever did — going into business with these guys. Granted: great guys, great business. I just so wanted to be back in the bar business."

Throwing caution to the wind, Frank left TV 5 and went to work at the Sports Corner fulltime. Such was his desire to be back in the bar business, he was willing to sacrifice roughly 50 percent of what he was earning at TV 5 for the pleasure.

"I thought," tells Frank. "Well, I'm going to have to change my lifestyle, but this is what I love."

Frank was determined to make it work and he did make adjustments to his lifestyle that would enable him to make the best of the $30,000 a year he was salaried at Sports Corner. He sold off some luxuries, including his boat and jet skis.

The Sports Corner was a busy place, offering not only a full bar and menu, but also regularly serving banquets on-site. Frank was happy to be a part of it all and brought the same bag of tricks to Sports Corner that had made Purcell's a hit — karaoke, 3rd and Short and a savvy promotional style. There was always something going on at Sports Corner, even if it was something strange.

Hermans invented promotional "games" to help lure in customers. One such game involved a urinal toss (a game similar to horseshoes which

The Hermans brothers with friends Paul and Wade Hendricks circa 1979. The Hermans family lived in Arkansas for only one year, but Frank recalls it being both the best and worst year of his life. It's the year he fell in love for the first time, but the girl — her name was Lucretcia — broke his heart. Pictured at the rear from back to front are Mike Hermans, Frank Hermans, Paul Hendricks, Wade Hendricks and Heath Hermans.

Frank outside the Chicago Theatre in 1989 where he first fell in love with 'Joseph and the Amazing Technicolor Dreamcoat.' Frank would see two performances of show, starring Donny Osmond, while in Chicago. His love for the musical had him jump at the opportunity to audition for a local production of the show in '94 at St. Norbert College. Frank was working at a bar called MVP Sports, which had locations in Naperville, Wis., and Carol Stream, Ill., at the time.

A band poster from one of Frank's earliest bands, Section 8, the follow up to his first band, Facked. The band featured the three Hermans brothers and guitarist Tom Keegan. Frank was enrolled at UWGB at the time while Heath was a sophomore in high school. The photo was taken in front of Lee's Cantonese House on E. University Ave., near the Hermans family home.

Frank and Joe Kiedinger pose for a photo in full costume before a performance of 'Joseph and the Amazing Technicolor Dreamcoat' in 1994. The two would create Frank's Dinner Theatre six years later.

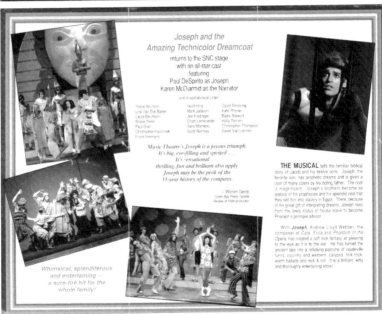

A summer theatre program from 'Joseph and the Amazing Technicolor Dreamcoat' in 1995 lists Frank Hermans and Joe Kiedinger as cast members. This performance at SNC kicked Frank's desire to perform into high gear. It was also during rehearsals that he 'faked' his way through the voice lessons, but learned a great deal by mimicking Scott Ramsay and Joe Kiedinger.

A newspaper announcement in 1994 introduces Frank Hermans as the newest member of the Van Boxtel sales team and mentions rock climbing as a hobby. Frank's approach to the sport earned him the nickname Hard Way Hermans.

After performing in 'Joseph and the Amazing Technicolor Dreamcoat,' Frank went on to land other roles in community theatre. Here he is in 1997 with April Strom, Douglas Durkee, Lana Kakuk and Susan Sherman in Evergreen Productions' Cole Porter Revue. Sherman would later appear as a cast member in Frank's Dinner Theatre.

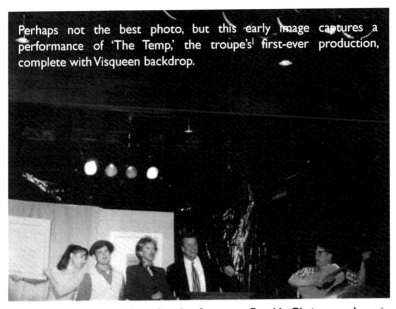

Perhaps not the best photo, but this early image captures a performance of 'The Temp,' the troupe's first-ever production, complete with Visqueen backdrop.

(Below) A promotional flyer for the first ever Frank's Christmas show in 2001, then-billed as 'Christmas at the Corner.' The Christmas show was a hit and has since become Frank's most well attended show. So popular is the Christmas show today that it is offered Tuesday through Saturday during the month of December and often requires the Meyer mezzanine to be opened to accommodate crowds. A Frank's Christmas is also the troupe's annual family-friendly performance, suitable for children of all ages.

This flyer also depicts the troupe's first logo, which utilized a Shakespearean figure that was later dropped, as the logo was too intricate to be embroidered on merchandise. Bassist Lee Starks came up with the replacement, which depicts Groucho glasses and is still in use today.

31

A MUSICAL COMEDY

Directed by Joe Kiedinger

The Cast

Darren Johnson: (Richard)
Darren is a graduate of St. Norbert College and a 4 Year member of the Swinging Knights. His previous credits include : Lion in the Wiz, Joe Cable in South Pacific, Will in Oklahoma , Great America Band, and Norman in Last of the Red Hot Lovers. He'd like to dedicate his performance to his grandmother who passed recently.

Frank Hermans: (Rooney)
Frank is a seasoned veteran of the Green Bay acting community. His credits include; Bob Cratchet in A Christmas Carol, a brother in Joseph and the Amazing Technicolor Dream Coat, and George in "It's a Wonderful Life."

Linda Wondrash: (Trudy Swan)
Linda has a n active role in the theatrical and radio community. Her credits include Sandy in "Grease," Andy in "Steppin' out with my Baby", Mary in "It's a Wonderful Life", and mother to Kyle and Loreli her two children. Linda is an announcer at 95.1 FM and works as an events coordinator for Q-90 FM.

Amy Riemer: (Tracy Swan)
Amy is a Graduate of St Norbert college and a former Swinging Knight. During her years there she had an active role in the Chamber and Vocal Ensemble Choirs. Amy has held numerous roles with Knight Theater and Summer Music Theater but her favorite roles include mother to her son Darien and fiancée to Jason.

Linda Feldmann: (Ms. Swanson)
Linda is an active musical theater performer. Her favorite roles include Anna in "The King and I", Sarah Brown in "Guys and Dolls", and the Baroness in "The Sound of Music" - all with Saint Norbert College Music Theater. In real life, Linda is a voice teacher, professional industrial film actress and print model.

Tony Boullire: (Scooter)
Tony is a graduate of St. Norbert College and was involved heavily in the Knight Theater. Tony played Mike in "Working", The Puppeteer in "Little Shop of Horrors", and had a supporting role in "Godspell." Tony was an active member of the Saint Norbert College Chamber Choir.

Joe Kiedinger: (The Temp)
Joe was a four year member of the St. Norbert College Swinging Knights, Chamber Choir and Vocal Ensemble. His Credits Include The Butcher in "Joseph and the Technicolor Dream Coat", Jinx in Forever Plaid, and was a lead production singer on Carnival Cruise Lines. Joe directs the choir program for Empire for the Arts and works in Marketing for WBAY.

Dave Zelzer: (Sound & Lights)
Dave is a relative newcomer to the theatrical world. He has spent the last five seasons working sound and lights for Evergreen Theater and was technical director for "A Christmas Carol." Dave is a production director for WDUZ/WQLH Radio and drums in a blues band on the weekends.

Holly Rottier: (Choreography)
Holly is a principal at a Pulaski elementary school. She has choreographed shows for Ashwaubenon, Southwest, and Luxemburg Casco High Schools. She has appeared in Saint Norbert College productions for the past seven years. She enjoys her free time with husband Jason and young son Cameron.

Kent Paulsen (Stage Manager)
Thanks to Kent for all his hard work and effort. His attention to detail has helped the show really come together.

Synopsis

"The Temp", a parody of both musical theater and business etiquette, takes place in an everyday office in an anywhere town . "Rooney", the office manager struggles to keep things on line while "Richard", the office slacker, pulls the plug on all advancement. The Swans, Scooter, and Ms. Swanson are trying to re- boot the company productivity but the work load has the entire office locked up!. Is it time to give the squeaky wheel the axe? Rooney knows Richards system is about to crash. Maybe it's time to call... *The Temp?"*

Special thanks to...

Managment & Staff for Putting up With This Crazy Cast!

A program for 'The Temp,' the first show performed by Frank's Dinner Theatre upon a makeshift stage located on the upper floor of the Sports Corner in De Pere. It was also the only script the troupe ever purchased from an outside source. Subsequent shows would utilize a review format, eventually introducing a full storyline in 2004 with 'Bandstand.' The troupe perfected the formula in 2005 with 'Beach Baby.'

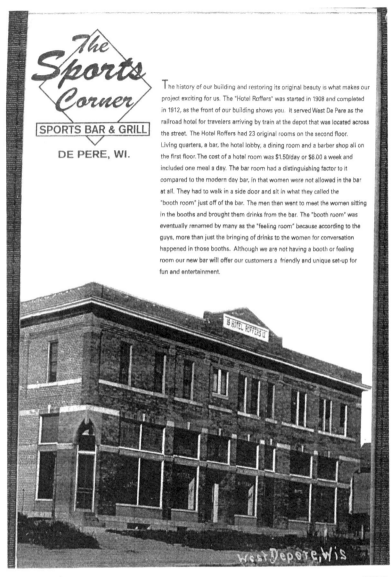

The history of our building and restoring its original beauty is what makes our project exciting for us. The "Hotel Roffers" was started in 1908 and completed in 1912, as the front of our building shows you. It served West De Pere as the railroad hotel for travelers arriving by train at the depot that was located across the street. The Hotel Roffers had 23 original rooms on the second floor. Living quarters, a bar, the hotel lobby, a dining room and a barber shop all on the first floor. The cost of a hotel room was $1.50/day or $6.00 a week and included one meal a day. The bar room had a distinguishing factor to it compared to the modern day bar, in that women were not allowed in the bar at all. They had to walk in a side door and sit in what they called the "booth room" just off of the bar. The men then went to meet the women sitting in the booths and brought them drinks from the bar. The "booth room" was eventually renamed by many as the "feeling room" because according to the guys, more than just the bringing of drinks to the women for conversation happened in those booths. Although we are not having a booth or feeling room our new bar will offer our customers a friendly and unique set-up for fun and entertainment.

The Sports Corner menu depicts the Roffer building as it was circa 1930. At one time, the hotel held a post office and store and was later used as an apartment building by students at nearby St. Norbert College. The building is the first home of Frank's Dinner Theatre. Performances were held on upper floor of the Sports Corner and early rehearsals took place in the basement.

33

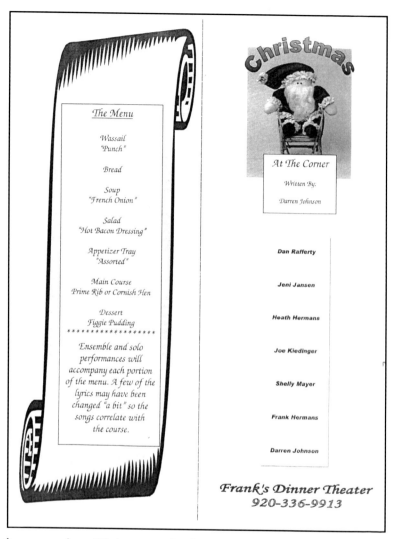

The Menu

Wassail
"Punch"

Bread

Soup
"French Onion"

Salad
"Hot Bacon Dressing"

Appetizer Tray
"Assorted"

Main Course
Prime Rib or Cornish Hen

Dessert
Figgie Pudding
* * * * * * * * * * * * * * * * * * *

Ensemble and solo
performances will
accompany each portion
of the menu. A few of the
lyrics may have been
changed "a bit" so the
songs correlate with
the course.

Christmas

At The Corner

Written By:

Darren Johnson

Dan Rafferty

Jeni Jansen

Heath Hermans

Joe Kiedinger

Shelly Mayer

Frank Hermans

Darren Johnson

Frank's Dinner Theater
920-336-9913

A program from 'Christmas at the Corner' includes a menu that offered the notorious Cornish hen as an entrée choice. The hens, much to Frank's dismay, were served to customers in varying degrees of rawness.

At The Corner "Cast"

Frank Hermans

Frank has been involved in the area theater for many years. He has had Major roles in It's a Wonderful Life, Scrooge, The Temp and most recently in our 60's & 70's reviews. Frank is the "founder of our feast" and quite honestly the reason we have a show at all. "God Love Em!"

Joe Kiedinger

Joe is the executive director of the theater and graduate of St. Norbert College. Joe was part of the St. Norbert Swinging Knights for four years and went on to Carnival Cruise Lines. In recent years he has opened Empire for the Arts and is an employee of WBAY. In the evenings Joe directs an all girls vocal group called "Showstoppers"...You should check these kids out... They're great!

Dan Rafferty

Dan is a former St. Norbert Swinging Knight, Football player and all around great guy. Dan jumped into our little group with both feet and has added a great deal. The poor guy even missed his work Christmas party! What a trooper...You're the goods Danny.

Darren Johnson

Darren is a former Swinging Knight and graduate of St. Norbert. His credits include Oklahoma, The Wiz, The Groovy 70's and a summer performances at Great America. Darren would like to send a special thank you out to his Family making a special trip to see him this holiday season. "I love you all very much".

Jeni Jansen

Jeni is the most recent addition to Frank's Dinner Theater. She is an accomplished singer / musician and "just likes to sing." Jeni was a standout in the 60's show and only seems to get better with each rehearsal and performance. We're lucky to have her.

Shelly Mayer

Shelly is a former Miss Green Bay and appeared in the Miss Wisconsin Pageant. A graduate of St. Norbert, she was a four year Swinging Knight and Chamber Singer. One of the most kind and sincere people we've ever met, Shelly carries the holiday spirit with her throughout the year.... And she's hot!

Heath Hermans

Heath has become a Frank's Diner Theater Regular. A jack of all trades, we have asked him to be a singer, drummer, actor, and he has come through without a word of complaint...well at least not any words we can mention. Thanks Heath.

Special Thanks to:

Tim our sound and light guy...If we sound great we say, "Thank you so much".. . Sound Bad, "It's the sound guy....He's new." We really couldn't do it without you.

Joe our spot light guy. He's there every show making sure no one on stage gets missed. Thank you for your support and all your effort Joe.

Denise, Keith, Frank Casey, Joe and all the staff at The Sports Corner for putting up with us!

SPORTS BAR & GRILL

DE PERE, WI.

The inside program lists the show's cast for the first-ever Christmas show. Special thanks is given to 'sound and light guy' Tim Funk, who now serves as the Meyer Theatre's technical director. His wife-to-be, Jeni, was a Frank's cast member.

SPORTS BAR & GRILL

DE PERE, WI.

FRANK'S DINNER THEATRE

Congratulations on making a FANTASTIC choice to experience
Frank's Dinner Theatre in 2001! This certificate will act as your
first step towards securing your seats for the dinner and show.
Please contact the Sports Corner at 336-9913 at your earliest
convenience to fill out a Dinner Theatre Package Confirmation
sheet. At that time we will need information from you including;
your name, address, phone number, who purchased the gift for you
if the show package is a gift, and type of package or shows included.
As a season ticket holder or pre-purchase ticket holder, you are
entitled to preferred seating and booking dates once a Confirmation
sheet is completed.

Once again we welcome you to the 2001 Dinner Theatre and look
forward to another great season of theatre at The Sports Corner Bar
& Grill.

FRANK'S DINNER THEATRE

Despite its modest beginnings, Frank's Dinner Theatre was a hit, evidenced
in part by this early offer to land season ticket holders who are offered
preferred seating as an enticement. Season ticket holders continue to be a
major part LMBF's success and now number 1,500. As it was then, season
ticket holders are still afforded certain enticements, such as reduced ticket
prices and a special performance given at an annual season ticket holder
party.

SPORTS BAR & GRILL

DE PERE, WI.

Frank's Dinner Theatre
2001 Show Package
Confirmation

Tuesday Meatloaf Pork Chops

SHOWS & DATES:

THE FABULOUS 50'S   February 14th-16th , 21st-24th

Tickets on sale to the public January 14th. Pre-purchase ticket holders &
season ticket holders pre-book dates January 7th-13th.

___ Dinner & Show $35.00   ___Show Only $20.00

THE GROOVY 70'S TAKE II   May 10th & 11th , 13th , 16th-18th

Tickets on sale to the public April 10th. Pre-purchase ticket holders &
season ticket holders pre-book dates April 3rd-9th.

___ Dinner & Show $35.00   ___Show Only $20.00

THOSE WERE THE DAYS (60'S)   July 15th-20th

Tickets on sale to the public June 15th. Pre-purchase ticket holders &
season ticket holders pre-book dates June 8th-14th.

___ Dinner & Show $35.00   ___Show Only $20.00

COUNTRY...DOWN ON THE CORNER   September 19th-23rd , 26th-29th

Tickets on sale to the public August 19th. Pre-purchase ticket holders &
season ticket holders pre-book dates August 12th-18th.

___ Dinners & Show $35.00   ___ Show Only $20.00

CHRISTMAS AT THE CORNER   December 1st , 2nd , 4th-7th

Tickets on sale to the public November 1st. Pre-purchase ticket holders &
season ticket holders pre-book dates October 25th-31st.

___ Dinner & Show $35.00   ___ Show Only $20.00

(Show times: Cocktails 6:00PM   Dinner 7:00PM   Show 8:00PM)

SEASON TICKET HOLDER PACKAGE

Dinner & Show tickets for all 5 shows. Season tickets on sale through Feb. 13th.

___ Season Ticket Package (Dinners & Shows) $162.00

(If booked for dinner & show, dinner selections will be required when booking your show dates.
Advance ticket holders receive preferred seating based on show dates and availability at the time
you call during the pre-book dates. WE RECOMMEND CALLING EARLY. Tickets are non-
refundable. If booking with a group that has people without pre-purchased tickets, preferred
seating will not be available for the whole group.)

NAME_____   PHONE_____

ADDRESS_____

_____   __visa/mc __cash __check

GIFTED FROM_____

A Frank's Dinner Theatre package confirmation sheet from 2001. In the
upper left the words 'Tuesday/Meatloaf/Pork Chops' are visible in Frank's
mother's handwriting. Karen was of invaluable aid while compiling this
book as she kept many of the images seen within.

A Message From Frank:

Thank you, Thank You, Thank You! If you are reading this, you are a big reason for our success, and the community's support of The Arts. Every individual you see on stage got his/her start right here in one of northeastern Wisconsin's local college or high school's theatre. Support The Arts in your schools. If it hadn't been for an abundance of area talent, the idea of a dinner theatre never would have come to fruition. A friend of mine (Joe Kiedinger) and I decided to turn an upstairs banquet room of the Sports Corner into a 100 person capacity theatre. The show was The Temp. The attendance was great, and our fledgling theater company was a hit. A local success story was born. I decided Frank's Dinner Theatre would become "all-original" and called on the writing talents of the cast. Initially, Darren Johnson and I came up with the silly bits, scripts and song structure. Later, Pat Hibbard was added to the mix, and Darren, Pat and I have been the writing force for the last two years. It's amazing that the first shows were written over a glass of suds and scratched on a bar napkin. The current team has turned it into a science. "The Team" would include every individual in the group as they all add to the final product of each review. A labor of love turned into a profession for most of Frank's Dinner Theatre Players and afforded this beautiful theatre. The ensemble will perform seven original shows this year and the theatre will welcome four additional performances by outside troupes as well. The theatre holds over 230 comfortably. It's tiered effect allows for excellent sight lines, state of the art sound lends to fantastic music, and the comedy will make you laugh, laugh and laugh. Enjoy something no other theatre is doing. It's all about trying Frank's Dinner Theatre... Why wouldn't cha?

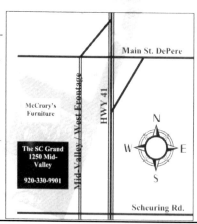

A message from Frank inside the 2003 SC Grand program mentions the troupe's early history, including the early shows being scripted on napkins, as well as credits Darren and Pat as part of the troupe's writing team. Also mentioned are the clear sight lines offered at the new tiered SC Grand, which Frank helped design. Around this time, all things were developing, including the programs, which were now printed mostly in color upon glossy paper.

Frank performing on the SC Grand stage in his first Elvis costume, which was made by Linda Groskopf. Linda is one of several seamstresses that create costumes for the troupe today.

Frank, dressed as a sailor, performs 'There's Nothing Like a Dame' from 'South Pacific' at the SC Grand.

A menu from the newly built SC Grand includes mention of both Larry McCarren's Locker Room and WFRV-TV 5. Only on rare occasions has Frank burned bridges, and he's often been able to incorporate friends from past endeavors into his newest projects.

THE SC GRAND — LARRY McCARREN'S LOCKER ROOM

BANQUET AND CONVENTION CENTER

APPETIZERS

FRENCH FRIES — $2.25
Try a tasty basket... Add nacho cheese .50

ONION RINGS — $3.00
Deep-fried to a golden brown

CHICKEN TENDERS — $4.50
Juicy white meat, lightly coated and seasoned...served w/ BBQ sauce or ranch dressing.

MOZZARELLA STICKS — $3.75
Wisconsin cheese lightly battered and served w/ marinara sauce

JALAPENO POPPERS — $4.00
Stuffed w/ cream cheese and fried to a golden brown. Served with ranch dressing or salsa

NACHOS — $3.25
Corn chips covered with nacho cheese, jalapeno peppers, served with salsa. Add sour cream .50

SAMPLE PLATTER — $6.50
Onion rings, chicken tenders, buffalo wings, mozzarella sticks, and jalapeno poppers served with assorted sides

BUFFALO WINGS — $3.50
12 juicy wings served plain (hot) or covered in hot sauce (even hotter)

NACHO SUPREME — $6.50
Taco meat, nacho cheese, lettuce, black olives, jalapeno peppers, green onions, tomatoes, and sour cream. Served over a mound of chips with salsa

---

GRILLED CHICKEN BREAST — $5.00
A 6oz. marinated boneless chicken breast served with lettuce and mayo on the side

CAJUN CHICKEN BREAST — $5.25
A 6oz. marinated chicken breast covered in spicy Cajun seasoning, served with lettuce and Cajun dressing on the side

SC GRAND "BIG DOG" — $4.00
The Sports Center's 100% pure beef hot dog. Chicago style (onions, tomatoes, relish and hot peppers) add .50

FISH FILLET — $4.75
Haddock deep-fried to a golden brown served with lettuce and tartar sauce... Add cheese .25

BLACK ANGUS CAJUN BURGER — $4.75
½ lb. Cajun spiced burger with pickles, onions and lettuce... served with Cajun sauce

THE BIG BLACK ANGUS — $4.50
Our BIG ½ lb. Lean Black Angus Burger served with pickles, onions and lettuce

BRATWURST — $4.00
Wisconsin's traditional football food. Served w/ kraut and onions

(ALL SERVED WITH FRENCH FRIES OR POTATO CHIPS)

Extras include: American, Swiss or cheddar cheese .10 mushrooms or tomatoes .25 bacon... .50 onions either raw or fried N/C

KIDS MENU

HAMBURGER BASKET — $2.75
Served with fries or potato chips and choice of drink... cheese .25

CHICKEN TENDER BASKET — $3.00
Served with fries or potato chips and choice of drink

HOT DOG BASKET — $2.50
Served with fries or potato chips and choice of drink

GRILLED CHEESE BASKET — $2.25
Served with fries or potato chips and choice of drink

The inside of the same menu.

The cover of the 2004 PlayFrank depicts images from the previous year.

A page from within the 2004 playbill illustrates the interior the SC Grand, which Frank helped design. Note the tiered level seating, which Frank borrowed from the Carlton West.

The cover and back page of the 2005 PlayFrank. Van Boxtel, where Frank had sold used cars, regularly took out the back page of Frank's programs.

A page inside the 2005 PlayFrank announces 'Beach Baby' as that year's fall show. The show, which featured music by the Beach Boys, Four Seasons and The Kingston Trio, looked much like a contemporary LMBF show and featured a complete story arc and marked a turning point in troupe history. The formula used in this show is still in use today.

The show also called for only two female roles, which left an angry Amy out of the cast. Her exclusion from this show has since become a humorous anecdote in Amy and Frank's relationship and is mentioned whenever Frank struggles to tell someone no.

The 2006 PlayFrank marked the final season the troupe would perform at the SC Grand.

In the annual Message from Frank inside the 2006 season program, the troupe's many changes are mentioned, which included the troupe's new name, taking on Pat Hibbard as a partner, the impending move to the Meyer Theatre and Amy's return. It also lists Shelly as a cast member for the last time, introduces Paul and is the first cast list that does not include Darren.

42

A mailer from the troupe's final season at the SC Grand. While the troupe continued to grow from their humble beginnings, mailers like this one are evidence of the hands-on approach the troupe took to marketing. Some 2,000 mailers like this were sent out that year, each with a stamp put there by a Let Me Be Frank's cast member.

A copy of the Meyer Theatre newsletter, Ovations, from 2005 announces Let Me Be Frank's debut show "Drive-In Movie," which ran for two weekends in June, as well as a Best of 2006 show slated for New Year's Eve. "Drive-In Movie" had been performed at the SC Grand the year before and was performed in 2006 at the Meyer as a gauge for both the Meyer board and Frank to determine future viability in the move. The show was a success.

43

This photograph was taken around Christmas of 1989 as a gift for their mother. From left are Heath, Mike and Frank. At this time, Frank had recently accepted a position at Fox Hills Resort and was moving ever closer to 'home.'

Frank, Mike and Heath show off their matching Elvis tattoos at the SC Grand bar. Frank bought the trio the ink at $50 apiece in 2003. This photo, taken in 2004, was given to their mother, Karen, for Christmas.
Photo by Credit Turba Photography

These early photographs capture the Hermans boys with their mother Karen.

This photo of Frank as a teenager has graced his mother's wall since 1982.

DOC'S LAFF FACTORY

123-1/2 Washington Street
Green Bay, Wisconsin

PRESENTS...

Nationally Touring Comedians

DRINK SPECIALS...

Just What The Doctor Ordered
46 oz. of Pure Pleasure! - One per human, please $10.00

Liver Buster
46 oz. of Pure Cirrhosis! - One per house call $15.00

My Wife Said I Could Only Have One
46 oz. of Liquid Courage! - One per human, please $10.00

P.S. The Glass Stays Here!

(Barkeep is more of a beer and shot
guy, but his Mom told him he had to
serve Fu-Fu drinks!)

Produced by:

LEE PRODUCTIONS
ENTERTAINMENT CONSULTANTS
Kenosha, WI • 414-657-4516

A mailer from Doc's Laff Factory, the follow-up to Doc's Comedy Club, boasts nationally touring comedians and offers 46-ounce drinks on the menu. These drinks, the Just What the Doctor Ordered, the Liver Buster and the My Wife Said I could Only Have One, were real drinks created by Frank Hermans.

FRI. & SAT., DEC. 1st & 2nd
Headlining: RUSS RIVAS

Through hard work and extensive touring, Russ proves to be a real crowd pleaser both on and off the stage. He brings with him a non-stop, high energy performance!
You may have seen Russ on *Short Attention Span Theater* - Comedy Central, *Comedy Compadres* - KTLA/TV, Los Angeles, and *Loco Slam* - H.B.O.
Come see why this act is a favorite from coast to coast.
Featured Act Robbie Roman

FRI. & SAT., DEC. 8th & 9th
Headlining: MIKE LUKAS

Mike enjoys playing the comedy club circuit and has performed at well over 20 renowned clubs, from *The Laugh Factory* in Chicago to *McCurdy's Comedy Club* in Sarasota. He has been a featured Comic on *"Stand-Up Stand-Up"* and *"Memphis Laffs"*, and has been principal actor or host in a variety of videos.
Featured Act Rich Clesen

FRI. & SAT., DEC. 15th & 16th
Headlining: RAY McCLONEY

This rising star, dubbed Fancy Ray McCloney, has opened for comedy greats Richard Pryor, George Wallace, and Tommy Chong.
His biggest accomplishment to date is as host of America's most entertaining cable talk show, *"Get Down With It!"*.
"...the man arrests your attention." says Brian Lambert of the *Saint Paul Pioneer Press*.
Featured Act Cris Patrick

FRI. & SAT., DEC. 22nd & 23rd
Headlining: DENNIS STALKER

Dennis placed 2nd in WI Funniest Person Contest. Here is what Pete Vertz of *Nights* and *Sounds* had to say " ...His twists on how he views certain sports, capped off with his own invented sport of cat bowling had me in stitches ." "Dennis Stalkar's likable personality and his views on being single, relationships, and marriage brings laughter to both sexes." James Wood - Madison State Journal.
Also Headlining...Shay Shay

FRI. & SAT., DEC. 29th & 30th
and SUN., DEC. 31st
Headlining:
REY GARIN

Rey is a resident of Chicago who has been performing all over the Midwest, including *Barrel of Laughs*, Oak Lawn-IL, *The Funny Firm*, Chicago-IL; several of the *Zanies* clubs ; *Comedy Cafe*, Milwaukee-WI; and even *The Oprah Winfrey Show*. He's not only a comedian, but has been writing comedy since 1981.
Featured Act Rich Brown

FRI. & SAT., JAN. 5th & 6th
Headlining: STEVE GOODIE

Headed for fame from the start as a class clown and leader of a neo-punk group known as *Imperial Trout Farm*, Steve was always making people laugh. However, 1986 found Steve floundering. That's when the voices started, saying "Get into comedy before you run out of gas money." In 1988 he became a regular at *Zanies*. His bizarre humor kept the audiences begging for more liquor, and the club owners grinning.
Featured Act Joe Bardetti

Inside the Doc's Laff Factory mailer, upcoming headliners are announced for the months of December through February. Many of the performers on the schedule, which included Larry Heagle, Spark Mann, Tom Naughton, Roger Radley, Ray 'Fancy Ray' McCloney and Brent Aitchison. Many of the talent that came through Doc's remain active performers to this day.

46

substituted horseshoes with urinal cakes and the stakes with a urinal). The game was apparently a hit during playoff football. Admittedly, they were "stupid games," but people seemed to like them and it kept things interesting. Like Purcell's, the Sports Corner was a hit, pulling in over 1.5 million dollars during its first year of operation.

Where does one go from a urinal toss? Naturally, live theatre.

Back in 1994, at the age of 30, Frank auditioned for a role in the summer music theatre production of "Joseph and the Amazing Technicolor Dreamcoat" at Saint Nobert College, under the direction of James and Dudley Birder. The musical was one of Frank's favorites. He had seen the production twice while living in Chicago years earlier. He knew the show like the back of his hand. The allure was great enough that he signed up to audition. It was his first audition in 12 years.

Herman impressed, and received a callback. He, along with two others, was up for the lead role: Paul DiSpirito and, fresh from entertaining passengers aboard Carnival Cruise Lines, Joe Kiedinger. Frank was humbled that he was being considered for the lead aside what he ascertained were more-professional performers. He knew the parts, yes. He knew he could sing, but the lead seemed too much. Not to worry, he didn't get it, not quite. At the second audition, he was asked if he knew the words to Reuben's country-esque song, "One More Angel in Heaven," which he did, he knew all the songs. He performed the song in his best country accent. Perhaps he did a little too well; he was offered the role of Reuben on the spot. Not the lead, but not bad for a guy that only auditioned for summer music theatre one time prior. His previous attempt was when he was 18 years old. He had received a callback then, too, but it was for the chorus and Frank was simply too cool for that. The part of Reuben, however, was prestigious enough that Frank went back to work and requested that Purcell's rework his schedule to allow him to attend rehearsals. They agreed.

Frank soaked up the "Joseph" experience like a sponge, taking note of everything and making the most of the connections he was making. He and Kiedinger became fast friends, and it was in preparation for Joseph that Frank received a professional crash course in vocal training.

While Frank could sing well enough to front a band or wow during karaoke night, he was unable to sight-read music. Wedged between what he describes as "two of the best tenors" in Joe Kiedinger and Scott Ramsay — the latter going on to fulfill an operatic career — Frank did his best to keep up with the pros, so to speak, by kind of faking it.

"I got to stand with these unbelievable singers, open my book, read music and sing. All I did was listen to those two guys and mimic what they did. That was all I did. They don't know how important they are to me or know what they did for me as a singer, but they made me sing like they did," says Frank.

Frank continued to audition for parts in community theatre. In doing so, he got to work with legendary director Herb Williams and landed the lead in Evergreen Productions' presentation of "It's a Wonderful Life" and was cast in a Cole Porter Revue titled "The Decline & Fall of the Entire World as Seen Through the Eyes of Cole Porter."

Frank had landed his role in the Cole Porter Revue as he had impressed with his look and his lead voice, but there was a problem. While Frank could sing lead, he was hopelessly lost with harmonies. When the show, which featured some 30 Porter songs, called for Frank to harmonize with his cast members, he didn't have a clue. Enter Kent Paulsen, who sat down with Frank and helped him learn all of his parts. When it came to vocal strength and tonality, Frank had learned on the fly by mimicking Kiedinger and Ramsay. But when it comes to learning to "hear" other performers and harmonize with them, Frank's first lessons came courtesy of Kent.

It was five years after "Joseph," sitting at the bar at Sports Corner that Frank suggested to Kiedinger that the two should start doing dinner theatre, utilizing the venue's banquet facility when it wasn't in use.

Recalls Kiedinger, "He approached me in November of 1999 and he said, 'I wanna start a dinner theatre and I want you to be executive director. I want you to come up with a show and find all the talent and I want you to be in it.'"

Kiedinger promptly informed Frank that live theatre venues topped the list of businesses most likely to fail in America, narrowly edging out restaurants for that dubious distinction. And here Frank wanted to combine the two?

Despite the warning, Frank pressed on and Joe suddenly had his hands full searching for a script, assembling the talent and acting for the then-unnamed theater group. That is, when he wasn't fulfilling his other duties as the fledgling troupe's executive director.

— A Message from Frank —
Getting back into the bar scene was so easy for me, the hard part was the money I was leaving on the table. I needed the excitement and sales were not doing it

for me. My thought was, "Do this for a couple of years and it will pay off in big dividends." And it sure did! If it wasn't for my partnership with the other owners of the Sports Corner and the vision of Joe Kiedinger, Frank's Dinner Theater would've been just a dream, I truly believe this. I'd probably still be doing karaoke at my brother Heath's bar for fun.

It was Ms. Janice Hirth, general manager of the Green Bay Radisson at the time, who let me try that acting thing again. I worked nights at Purcell's in the Radisson, and how could I do a musical working that schedule? Janice let me do "Joseph and the Amazing Technicolor Dreamcoat" in 1994. I adjusted my schedule to accommodate rehearsals and performances. It was at this show I met one of my best friends, Joe Kiedinger. Big kudos, Janice! The bar biz was not completely filling my need to perform, although Purcell's was a bit of acting all the time.

Joe Kiedinger was the man for Frank's Dinner Theatre at this time; his role was that of Executive Director of Frank's Dinner Theatre. Joe's duties were all encompassing from scripts to cast. He did this all while working full time at WBAY-TV where he was fast becoming a well seasoned ad executive. Joe has always impressed me by his attention to detail and his creative genius. I truly believe I would not have what I have today if it wasn't for this gifted man. If you read this, Joe, thank you!

A TEMPORARY THING OR TRASH BAG THEATRE

Undeterred, and not one to be derailed by silly things like facts, Frank's gears began to grind and things were full steam ahead. At the time, the plan was to do *real* musical theatre and that meant buying the rights to shows created by outsiders to perform.

Frank set about traveling, including out of state, to catch dinner theatre and take notes in preparation for what would they were calling Frank's Dinner Theatre.

It may come as a surprise to some, as it's become difficult to recognize a distinction between Frank the man and Frank the brand, that it was Joe, not Frank, who came up with the name Frank's Dinner Theatre. In fact, for a man that admits an early ambition to "become a star," Frank has a way of steering the spotlight away from himself or, at least, dragging others into it with him.

"I think Frank wanted to call us Nicolet Players," recalls Kiedinger.

At hearing Joe's suggestion to call the troupe Frank's Dinner Theatre, Frank returned the suggestion with "How about we call it Frank and Joe's?"

Joe, who was and still is a marketing expert, knew better. "I thought it was funny because he was at Purcell's and he was bigger than life at Purcell's. He's on the radio with his loud ads and he was at Doc's and he was always a front man and I thought, 'What a wonderful personality. This guy is so bigger than life. We've gotta use his name.'"

The name not only put the larger-than-life Hermans with all his promotional prowess into the spotlight, but it also reflected the sort of theatre the troupe would offer. It wasn't Shakespeare. It was everyman's theatre, with a brand of comedy best served with a Miller Lite (or six). The name was a nod to the working class and meant to evoke images akin to Joe's Diner, Al's Auto or Dick's Hardware.

With a name now in place, Joe set about his other executive duties. Frank may have been guilty of dropping the bulk of the legwork for his idea in Joe's lap, but he at least picked the right guy for the job. Joe had connections.

Through a friend, Joe was connected with Minneapolis playwright Brian Kelly. Kelly had recently completed writing a musical called "The Temp," with music by Todd Price. It was a comedy that had a shared lineage with the heroic western, but took place in an office setting. The following synopsis, as it appeared in the original Frank's Dinner Theatre program, complete with grammatical errors, read thusly:

"The Temp", a parody of both musical theater and business etiquette, takes place in an everyday office in an anywhere town. "Rooney", the office manager struggles to keep things on line while "Richard", the office slacker, pulls the plug on all advancement. The Swans, Scooter, and Ms. Swanson are trying to re- boot the company productivity but the work load has the entire office locked up!. Is it time to give the squeaky wheel the axe? Rooney knows Richards system is about to crash. Maybe it's time to call... **"The Temp?"**

In searching for a cast, Joe would lean on the connections he'd forged in the local theatre community. He had appeared in 12 musicals at St. Norbert College since the age of 5, and he used his connections, especially those made with the Swinging Knights, of which he was a member, to field a team for Frank's Dinner Theatre. He brought in Darren Johnson,

Linda Wondrash, Linda Feldmann, Tony Boullire, Dave Zetzer, Holly Rottier-Prast, Kent Paulsen and a 25-year-old Amy Riemer to serve as cast and crew for the troupe's first production.

So strong were Joe's connections at St Norbert's, the school even let them borrow a stage — one of the troupe's few items that wasn't makeshift. The remainder of the troupe's legitimate effects were comprised of a PA system with corded microphones and lighting rig used by 3rd and Short. Frank recalls the corded mics being problematic onstage as they caused the troupe to get creative with its choreography.

Everything else for that first show was done on a shoestring budget or no budget at all. Office props and wardrobe came courtesy of visits to local thrift stores. The Sports Corner was busy and that was good for business, but it left the troupe without a proper rehearsal space, so the troupe utilized the Sports Corner's dingy basement, reciting lines while sitting atop beer crates, singing among the beer kegs and assorted oddities that end up in a barroom basement. When it came time to take their show upstairs, aluminum foil was placed over the windows to dim the area and turn the upstairs banquet facility into something like a proper theatre. And lacking a proper curtain system, the troupe instead used black polyurethane Visqueen — essentially garbage bag sheeting — as a backdrop at their early performances.

"Some theatres were nifty, nifty, nifty; ours was hefty, hefty, hefty," says a grinning Kiedinger.

Even Press-Gazette critic Warren Gerds took notice, drawing a parallel between the production's title and the theatre itself noting, "'Temp' could also apply to the stage. It's in a corner of a banquet room, and it is both temporary and makeshift — like so many first-time ventures."

"Yeah, we were trash bag theatre in those days," admits Frank.

Despite the lack of grandeur, the show, which opened on a Monday night, received a positive response, both from the crowd and from Gerds — the latter gave the show three of four stars and stated that the cast was "bright and lively" and "over the top."

Not bad for trash bag theatre.

The show did well enough that the troupe wasted little time in preparing a second show. Frank and Joe set out to find a new script. Among those they considered was a script called "Monkey Business," written by the brother of local insurance agent John Boland, but nothing leapt out at them.

Frank and Joe spent more time at the Sports Corner pondering their next move, perhaps thinking inspiration could be found at the bottom of the next empty pitcher of beer. Eventually the duo took a closer look at what they really needed to put together a show and became convinced that everything they needed was right under their noses.

"We realized when looking at 'The Temp,' it just seemed kind of easy," recalls Frank. "We figured we could write our own dialog."

After all, "The Temp" may have been an original creation, but that didn't mean it didn't borrow from other sources. The show incorporated familiar pop elements that included a sword fight (with office laser pointers instead of swords), a spoofing of the "I'm Flying" scene from the 1997 hit film "Titanic" and even a villain character a la Phantom of the Opera that resided in the office storeroom. It wasn't all that complicated.

In realizing they could write their own material, Frank's Dinner Theatre had decided to work smarter not harder. Instead of focusing their search for a new show outwardly, they began to look inwardly.

"We had so much right in front of us," says Frank. "I mean, just in Joe, he was a wealth of knowledge."

Again, Joe's history with the Swinging Knights would come into play as many numbers from previous Knights' shows would wind up in what Frank's Dinner Theatre were calling "The Groovy '70s."

It's been said that good artists borrow and great ones steal. According to Frank he was the latter. "We, pretty much, ripped off all the stuff from Swinging Knights and put it in the show. That's pretty much what it was. When I sit and think about it, we stole everything."

"I remember people applauding us for our use of medleys after the show. They'd ask how we had come up with such a great Beatles medley or Supremes medley. The truth was we didn't."

Well, not everything was stolen; some of it was simply borrowed. Again using what was right at hand, 3rd and Short were called in to cover the musical duties, performing '70s songs that had long been in the band's repertoire. The troupe's vocalists had no sheet music or notes to work from and would learn their songs by following along to the original recordings and following along.

Frank and Joe set to writing out the new show's script on napkins at the Sports Corner bar over four pitchers of beer. There is some lack of consensus as to the number of napkins. Frank insists the entire script required the use of seven napkins. Joe remembers five. There is no argument over the four pitchers of beer.

Regardless, this new show hadn't the MacGuffin that "The Temp" had. There was no linear storyline to speak of. "The Groovy '70s" was instead a mishmash of bits and skits that played to the cast's strengths and were gathered together loosely by a time period. It was a variety show, set as one might expect, in the 1970s.

Impersonations were the order of the day and Frank's early shows delivered, serving up healthy doses of Olivia Newton John, Johnny Cash, Dean Martin, Willie Nelson, The Smothers Brothers and more. Some impersonations were better than others.

"I did Stevie Wonder," says Joe Kiedinger, who shares little to no resemblance to the Motown great. "I wore an Afro. I was terrible at mimicking Stevie Wonder. I'd say, 'How ya doing?' — that sounding nothing like him, but then I'd sing one of his songs and it was fun."

Mr. Wonder didn't make it into "The Groovy '70s," but many other stars did, including Don McLean, Joni Mitchell, Neil Diamond, The Eagles, Janis Joplin, Simon & Garfunkel, The Jackson 5, Pat Benatar and more.

It was during "The Groovy '70s" show that Frank impersonated Elvis for the first of what would be many times thanks to some encouragement after a karaoke session. "I had no idea I could impersonate Elvis; that was the first time I had ever done an Elvis song publically."

Also a first, "The Groovy '70s" marked Frank's first public appearance as Cher. He recounts being on a trip to Las Vegas with Ed Van Boxtel as part of a sales reward trip that he first realized he could do a pretty good impression of the Goddess of Pop. He was sitting in the front row during the tribute show Legends in Concert when Frank caught "Cher's" attention.

"I was sitting in the front row and she noticed I was singing along to 'Gypsies, Tramps and Thieves.' She came over and handed me the microphone and I finished the last half of the song."

Frank nailed it and the impromptu performance was a hit with the crowd. "I had no idea I could sing like her, but Cher is very similar to Elvis in the way they both have the roll to their voices when they sing."

"The Groovy '70s" ran for seven nights in May of 2000. Much like its predecessor, "The Temp," the operation was a success. Critic Warren Gerds was again impressed with the fledgling troupe. He applauded the show for not only bringing back the music of the '70s, but also the variety show format that was so popular during that decade. He went on to say the show was "infectiously fun" and "a celebration of some of the best moments of the time."

The critic called the troupe's rendition of "I've Got You Babe" in which Frank at 6-foot 3-inches tall played the part of Cher, while Darren played the diminutive Sonny Bono from his knees "outrageously funny." He awarded the show three and a half of four stars.

Those early productions were created with a threadbare budget, but that didn't mean the productions didn't bring in money. Some of that money always made it back to the cast. Frank has always hung his hat on the belief that performers needed compensation for their work.

"It was important to me. Nobody, at least in Green Bay, was paying people to do live theatre," says Frank. "I knew how much work went into performances. I remembered doing summer theatre and we'd rehearse for a month, every day, six hours a day, but at the end of it, all the cast got was applause. Applause is great, but I felt all these people needed more than applause."

A ticket for dinner and a show was $30. Fifteen dollars of every paid ticket went to the Sports Corner to cover food and dining expenses, leaving $15 of every ticket to come back to Frank's Dinner Theatre. Four dollars of each ticket went toward marketing costs and $11 of every ticket came back to the troupe proper. As the executive director, Joe was given 25 percent of that take and the remainder was divvied out to the cast. Frank, despite performing, did not take a cut.

While the profits from the shows wouldn't have any of the cast rushing to purchase real estate on the sunny side of St. Simons Island, it was welcomed.

"I was just thrilled to be getting paid," says Amy Riemer. "Up until that time, I was doing a lot of things, but I was doing them for free."

Riemer wasn't much for partying, and, as the only mother in the troupe, the money undoubtedly came in handy. But for the many in the cast, it was easy come easy go. The money earned was spent just as quickly as it had come in, and much of it on booze.

"Rehearsing and performing in those days it was just big party. That's all it was," admits Frank. "Sure we would learn our lines and our songs, do our choreography, but we had beers before the show, we had beers during the show. It was almost like going out.

"It was weird having people come to pay $30 to come see us. We couldn't believe it; the place would sell out. And we were just pounded; it was drunk-fest."

The troupe did little to hide their indulgences. By show's end, a line of empty Miller Lite bottles would sit atop a brick ledge behind the band's drum kit, in plain few of the audience. In those days, Frank didn't see anything especially wrong with the troupe's bacchanal ways. After all, he was a bar manager, but not everyone was impressed, including mom.

Recalls Frank: "I'll never forget my mom saying to me after the show, she said, 'Beaver, do you think it's a good idea having all those beer bottles on stage?'"

That may have got him thinking, but it didn't instantly elicit changes.

Frank admits that performers were frequently drunk — well, the boys were, anyways — while on stage during the troupe's early years. He calls it a "practiced behavior" that in most instances didn't affect the final outcome. The troupe wrote, practiced and performed its productions while often under the influence. There was perhaps collective tolerance at work in those early days, or it could have simply been denial.

"Back in the day, it *seemed* I could sing and perform just as well while hammered as I could do when I wasn't," says Frank. "Obviously, that's not the case."

For Frank, a self-described "happy drunk," having a few too many before or during a performance melted away inhibitions. What may have been scripted as a PG show might fade a little closer to a PG-13 show after a couple of drinks.

Fair enough had that been the only consequence of drink, but not everyone handles the creature the same way. Some people get downright mean when drinking, others unreliable and some both. But for the time being, it was all in fun. It wouldn't be until later that, when things got really serious one might say, that addressing alcohol usage would become necessary to the troupe's future.

— A Message from Frank —

When we did shows at the Sports Corner there was a lot of costume changes (the costumes came from Dreams Come True in Allouez). We would change in the same hall where the food was served, girls would use the bathroom and us men would dodge chicken and steak entrees while changing. Not one to be afraid of his own skin, let's just say the girls probably saw a little too much of my derriere in the beginning.

It was my brilliant idea to use Visqueen for the backdrop. Not the brightest bulb on the tree that day. The plastic sheeting was glossy and gave off a shiny effect. Needless to say, it lasted one show, but the aluminum foil on the windows continued, kind of Howard Hughes-y.

A BIGGER BOAT OR WOULD YOU LIKE TO SUPERSIZE IT?

From a financial perspective, Sports Corner was a success, pulling in over $1.5 million during its first year of operation. With the venue's banquet area completely booked and Frank's Dinner Theatre gaining momentum, an expansion seemed a no-brainer. Plans to build a second, larger venue began to take shape. They would call it the SC Grand.

Building the SC Grand from scratch meant Sports Corner owners could be picky in designing the new venue. Frank saw it as an opportunity not only to tailor the new venue to his theatre group, but also to his old friend Larry McCarren.

Frank's input on the project was an amalgam of the theatre designs he'd seen in places like Chanhassen, Minn., Branson, Mo. and Chicago, Ill., while traveling to research other dinner theatres. He threw in a little bit of Green Bay's Carlton West for good measure.

While on the road researching venues, he recalls inadvertently receiving some advice from the theatre troupes he'd see. One owner, who ran a theatre in Chicago, told him plainly, "Don't do this; it's the worst business to get into."

Frank didn't listen.

"At that time, we were all dreamers. We were at capacity with the Sports Corner, doing nearly $2-million a year and unable to add any more shows to the schedule because we were completely booked. What else could we do? We had to go forward. The sky was the limit," says Frank.

To get McCarren on board, Frank drew from his past experience working with McCarren's show at Purcell's, and insisted the new SC Grand be as television-friendly as possible. McCarren, upon inspection, was impressed and did relocate his show to the Grand, where he would continue to broadcast from until Frank's departure from the venue in 2006.

The significantly larger SC Grand Banquet and Convention Center, located at 1250 Mid Valley Drive in De Pere, opened its doors to customers in September of 2001. This new location could seat more patrons — 220 versus the Sports Corner's 132 — and allowed more and larger wedding and banquet parties to be booked. It also gave Frank's Dinner Theatre an opportunity to perform on Fridays and Saturdays. Up until this time, Frank's troupe operated Sunday through Thursday, leaving Fridays and Saturdays open to cater to banquet hall renters.

That year, Frank's was offering five shows. The earlier three shows, "The Fabulous '50s," "The Groovy '70s Take II" and a '60s-themed show "Those Were the Days" were performed at the Sports Corner. That left the remaining two shows, a country-themed show "Down on the Corner" and the troupe's first Christmas show entitled "Christmas at the Corner" to be performed at the new SC Grand. The latter would become a Frank's staple, earning the troupe its first four-star review and kicking off what would become the troupe's most well attended annual show.

The new SC Grand may have been more accommodating, but there still wasn't enough room for Frank's needs. It wasn't uncommon for two weddings and a Frank's Dinner Theatre show to go on simultaneously at the Grand, and Frank admits to pushing the venue's occupancy, even making a game of sorts out of how many extra people he could pack into the venue — sometimes pushing the building's capacity to nearly 280 people.

Such occasions created a frantic scenario for Frank who had to juggle performing in the show, serving food to customers and checking on his wedding parties in the same evening.

And despite its design improvements over the Sports Corner, one detail had been forgotten: sound proofing. True, large sections of the facility could be sectioned off using temporary wall dividers, but those weren't soundproof. Frank recalls performing on stage while the neighboring wedding party's DJ launched into Madonna's "Celebrate" at deafening volume. The cast had no choice but to adlib or make mention of the raucous during the performance.

To combat this, Frank's longtime soundman, Tim Funk, created carpeted foam sections that had to be manually installed along the wall dividers, but with no sound barriers installed in the ceilings, it wasn't a perfect solution to the problem.

Also of concern was the venue's food. Frank recalls the turnover being high among the Grand's cooks and proof of the fact occasionally found its way onto the plates of patrons. Frank recalls a holiday show that featured Cornish game hen on the menu. The evening was a disaster with nearly three of every 10 birds served noticeably undercooked.

"Whoever was our cook at the time, well, they should have been fired. It was a disaster."

Not all the food must have been a disaster, however, as critic Warren Gerds made mention of it in his review of the troupe's first show at the new venue, "Down on the Corner," which ran during the last two weekends in September and the first weekend of October 2001. The country-themed performance also included a country inspired meal — Gerds recommended the barbecued ribs.

The troupe's synopsis of the show, complete with Frank's developing promotional prowess, read thusly:

This show is "countrier" than a turnip green! Now that's country! Frank's Dinner Theater presents a brand new country music review. The best of the old and some of the new hits of all your favorite artists. A "hoot hollerin, rip roarin" good time had by all. If you haven't been to one of the shows you need to make plans to go! Any review this group has gotten for an original show has been no less than three and a half out of four stars! The theater is located inside the newly built SC Grand "home of the Larry McCarren Locker Room Show" and promises a great experience. The guys in the cast are goofy, crazy, and sometimes dumber than a bag of hammers but the girls are prettier than a new pair of snow tires! So come on down to the SC Grand! Franks Dinner Theater and a brand new Country show!

As for the show, Gerds made special note of Frank's performance, calling him "totally outlandish" and "spectacularly funny" in two of his routines. One had Frank playing the part of a John Wayne inspired plumber sporting a low lying tool belt while performing "Big Bad John" — John in this instance being a toilet. In the other routine, Frank played the role of a female semi truck driver and sang "I'm Driving a Truck with High Heels On."

Gerds said that everything was a step up for the troupe, saying "Audiences will love the show, like the place and enjoy the meal, for which plates keep coming until you call it quits."

The show also featured a patriotic closing number — Elvis Presley's "An American Trilogy." It was a fitting end to the troupe's first performance in the wake of the Sept. 11, 2001, attacks, which were just days old at the time. Some may have felt the performance was inserted after Sept. 11, but the selection had been written into the script since its inception.

Frank and company would go on to perform 32 shows at the new venue, but a climate of change was in the air, beginning early in the 2002 season with the amicable departure of Joe Kiedinger, who left to meet the demands of his burgeoning marketing company, which continues to serve area clients to the present day.

Joe's departure left a hole in the troupe's writing sessions, leaving Frank and Darren to handle the majority of the show's writing duties with troupe newcomer Pat Hibbard.

Pat Hibbard and Frank Hermans seemed destined to collide at some point in history no matter what — their paths crossing innumerable times before the two finally connected creatively.

Both had attended UWGB at the same time, Pat was a year ahead of Frank, but the two never really connected.

Both were performing in bands on the local club circuit, but again, didn't fully connect.

The two admit to knowing *of* the other without actually knowing the other.

Pat Hibbard was a cancer survivor and had successfully beaten non-Hodgkin's lymphoma in his late teens. By 1983 or so, Hibbard was heavily invested in music and had become a sort of celebrity in the local music scene. Pat was busy with multiple bands, including The Blitz (with current LMBF keyboardist Tony Pilz). The Blitz cut an album in Kansas City and garnered the attention of a subsidiary of CBS before fading away. Frank recalls catching Hibbard's gigs and even being intimidated by his "rock star" status.

"I'd go to see his shows and here's this guy with this long hair and crazy eyes; he had evil eyes. And he can sing like a motherfucker," says Frank of Hibbard who's on stage wardrobe embodied the hair metal makeover, complete with spandex and makeup.

At some point down the line, Hibbard's involvement with local bands slowed and he purchased a music agency and set to work lining up gigs for local bands as Direct Hit Productions. One of Direct Hit's acts: 3rd and Short.

"I didn't really know Frank, but I knew he was a blast," says Hibbard.

As part of Pat's duties as an agent, he would put together promo kits for the bands he represented. 3rd and Short had no promotional material at the time, but that was about to change.

"As an agent, I tried to put out decent promo for these bands and Frank had nothing. So, we put something together with half-assed pictures and I suggested, 'Why don't we put on there some quotes by club owners?'"

Frank was happy to oblige and offered the following endorsements from club owners:

-- "Almost as good as the band we had last week."
-- "Is that what it's supposed to sound like?"
-- "The best band in their price range."

Hibbard was impressed with the humorous marketing approach. He was also impressed with the band's results … no matter where he booked them.

"I could book these guys at a shitty bar and they'd kill. I could book them at a casino and they'd kill," says Hibbard. "It didn't seem to matter where I booked them, they'd kill."

It's at that time that Pat realized there was something to Frank and 3rd and Short. They had something going for them, but Pat couldn't quite put his finger on exactly what it was … and he'd had a chance to see the group in action up close, making things even more perplexing.

"I had filled in with 3rd and Short and played a couple of gigs with them," says Hibbard. "Super unorganized! I grew up playing in bands and you had a set list and I asked them, 'What are we doing?' They said, 'Everything's in E, follow Tommy for the changes. Oh, by the way, we have another show tonight.' That's how unorganized it was."

Organizational skill wasn't the band's strong suit, nor was it the reason the band was so popular. At the core of its charisma was frontman Frank Hermans.

"Frank can stand in front of anybody — you still see it now — it doesn't matter: gray hairs or a young audience, he's comfortable. And if he isn't comfortable, he sure as hell looks like he is. I was kind of drawn to it even then," recalls Pat.

Fast forward to the year 2000. Frank is working at Sports Corner and Frank's Dinner Theatre is on the verge of losing one of their own. Bassist Lee Starks, who was with 3rd and Short and its precursor, the Rude Boys, as well as Frank's Dinner Theatre is having trouble juggling family life with the demands of performing. Lee holds a somewhat unsung role in Frank's Dinner Theatre history as the troupe's first de facto marketing expert. He was responsible for creating the troupe's first logo and website and opening its first Facebook account.

Pat is selling advertising for Cumulous Broadcasting and Sports Corner is one of his clients. He's present — complete in suit and tie instead of spandex and lipstick — for a radio broadcast from Sports Corner by Packer Billy Lyons. Frank approached Pat and asked him if he might be interested in performing in the troupe's next show?

His response: "Yeah, what does that pay?"

Pat began rehearsing with the troupe and the show went off without a hitch, but Pat — who had studied theatre — saw potential for the troupe moving forward and used his enthusiasm to "weasel" his way into the writing sessions.

— *A Message from Frank* —

We all had struggled on what to call our newest venture on Mid Valley Road. Some of the names suggested were Frank's Dinner Theatre (which I liked the best but later was glad it wasn't used) and Sports Corner West. I believe it was building partner Scott Van Den Heuvel who came up with SC Grand, which stands for Sports Corner Grand, brilliant! I really loved designing the new cabaret stage, I was such a rookie but I had this idea from the Carlton West days of booths and levels. Booths never made it in the design but the levels did. I also designed the big sign in front of the property, I had worked at Jones Sign and used a little of my expertise to design it.

I remember many times at the SC Grand bartending before the show, serving dinner and getting on stage 10 minutes later smelling of the night's fare. This was the norm every night at the Grand. The worst was telling the DJs and bands in the other rooms to keep it down till 10 p.m., most listened, some could give a shit. At times our LMBF band would start playing the same song the DJ or band was playing in the other rooms. All of our customers never complained because we made a joke of it, but inside, I was just boiling and let say some of those DJs and bands really got an ear full after the show.

Pat and I became fast friends and clicked right away. Our writing styles were very different but worked well together. Pat or RainPat as I call him, is an encyclopedia of Americana and music, I, on the other hand, was really good at bullshitting.

TO BE OR NOT SO MUCH OR MAKING LEMONADE IN GREENER GRASS

There was no doubt that Franks Dinner Theatre was a hit and the new venue, even if not perfect, was a step in the right direction for the troupe. In its first year at the SC Grand, Frank's Dinner Theatre brought in $1.8 million, which accounted for more than half of the venue's revenue that year, but not everyone was in love with Frank and company.

Critic Warren Gerds, in his first review of the troupe said that Frank's was a "let-your-hair-down type of show." And so it still is, but that isn't to say that thought wasn't given to changing things up in favor of a more "legitimate" type of theatre.

Whatever Frank and company was doing during those early years, it was working. Undoubtedly, Frank and Joe made a great team. As friends, performers and writers, they made a great duo, but that isn't to say they weren't without their differences.

When it came to comedy, or more specifically, the type of comedy that would find its way to the stage, this is perhaps where the friends differed the most.

Frank's comedy was blue comedy. Not to be confused with blue-collar comedy. Frank preferred being off-color, a little crude and leaning toward vulgarity.

"I think Kiedinger wanted everything really clean," recalls Hibbard. "He wanted everything above board and the comedy to rely on innuendo and then you've got Frank and he's the king of fart jokes."

Admits Frank: "Farts were funny in my household. Not to mom but to my dad."

This type of humor was in contrast to Joe's cleaner, G-rated slapstick variety. Joe was a professionally trained performer. He had received proper instruction in theatre, voice, etc. And while Frank's Dinner Theatre was never in search of Shakespearean heights, it may have been below Joe's abilities.

"His blue got to a point where it was dumb. It wasn't even funny to me," says Kiedinger. "Like, you should imply breasts, you shouldn't just say it."

Perhaps the biggest opponents to the troupes blue ways were Joe's parents, but they weren't the only ones who found the shows lowbrow.

Many within the area's theatre community dismissed Frank's Dinner Theatre as being illegitimate; some went so far as to publicly ridicule the troupe. Others, most infuriatingly of all, impetuously bashed the troupe without having ever seen a show.

To Frank, an avid supporter of community theatre till this day, the criticism struck a nerve. Whether his detractors thought they were upholding some form of theatrical integrity or were simply jealous of the troupes success, Frank admits to taking some of it to heart.

One particularly damning instance occurred on Facebook. A local thespian warned that if anyone was interested in garbage theatre they'd need look no farther than to hack performer Frank Hermans and his troupe.

Frank has an interesting method of dealing with criticism. Whether from his years in the service industry or just a part of his makeup, Frank wants to change people's minds.

It would be curious to witness the reaction of one of Frank's detractors when they receive a phone call or an email from Frank himself, making apologies for their dissatisfaction before seeking a way to make things right. Although quaint, this is generally how Frank handles his detractors. Frank mentions a genuine "desire to make things right when people aren't happy."

To this day, it isn't uncommon for Frank to describe himself as a hack. And while a self-deprecating Frank may not have had collegiate theatrical training, others in his troupe did. And Frank wasn't the only one affected by the criticism.

Pat Hibbard recalls his anger when one of his former professors made disparaging remarks about LMBFs to his students.

As part of the course curriculum, students were instructed to go out and see area shows as part of a set design class, but were told that Let Me Be Frank shows didn't count.

Hibbard once confronted his former professor on this point and was told LMBF was omitted because they didn't use real sets.

Hibbard conceded the point, but responded, "You don't qualify it that way to your students. You just flat out tell your students that Let Me Be Frank Productions doesn't count."

While negative criticism never made up the bulk of the response from any show Frank and company performed, Frank says it wasn't uncommon to receive a letter or two after the run of each show by an angry customer saying they'd never bring their family to another show. In his typical small town fashion, Frank took many of them seriously and responded to many of them personally to try and explain himself. Frank, often very much a glass-half-full persona, nearly let the minority that made up his naysayers get the better of him.

His irritation grew to such an extent, he considered making changes to appease his detractors.

"I actually started thinking that I was going to clean up my act," admits Frank.

Surprisingly, encouragement to remain true to his style came from a most unlikely source.

"I didn't like being a part of the blue," says Kiedinger. "But when I left I told Frank, 'That is your brand. Whatever you're doing is working.'"

He was right. The troupe's brand of humor may not have been for everyone, but it was working. In fact, it worked well enough that other theatre groups — one from Oregon, the other from Canada — approached Frank's Dinner Theatre interested in franchising the troupe's performances.

Yes, the troupe's formula was working, and while the area's "legit" performers had only applause to look forward to, Frank and company were doing something they loved and making a little money doing it. Changing wasn't in the cards, at least not for this crew.

"Even if we made a conscious effort to make the show really, really clean, at some point everyone of us slides into the easy fart or dirty joke," says Hibbard.

"We've always taken crap for how blue we are. That's one thing that we've hung our hat on. We've stayed true to our humor. It's not highbrow. It never has been, nor have we ever claimed it to be," proclaims Frank.

Frank recalls some advice that comedian Nick DiPaolo gave him back during the days of Doc's Comedy Club. Nick said, "You're going to piss off 10 percent of the people with your act, but the other 90 percent are going to love you."

For better or for worse, Frank wasn't bowing to the 10 percent. In fact, Frank and company were about to double down on their brand of comedy.

— A Message from Frank —

I love "Saturday Night Live," I love Cheech and Chong, I love Carol Burnett and I love "Blazing Saddles." That's the type of comedy we do in our shows. Our comedy punches you in the face and dares you to laugh. Some people say we are PG-13 or rated R. Well, those people have never seen "Rent," "The Book of Mormon" or "The Best Little Whorehouse in Texas." We have some really talented comedians who can sing the daylights out of any song and then make you fall over with laughter. The brand works! In 2009 we had 700 season ticket holders; today we have over 1,500. We continue to grow every year and it still amazes us that they (you) keep coming. We do maintain a completely clean, innuendo free Christmas show. Even the kiddies can come see that one.

BLUE TIMES TWO OR
DOES THIS TASTE SOUR TO YOU?

In July of 2004, LMBFs unveiled "Bandstand," which was a digression from the troupe's normal revue show. "Bandstand," featured a more structured story arc, which starred Frank in the role of Frank Fontaine, the host of, you guessed it, "Frank Fontaine's Bandstand."

The show's highlights included Pat Hibbard stepping up from usual bass guitar duties into a prominent lead role, complete with terrible comb-over wig and a series of commercials, most notably one that had Fontaine endorsing Niagara starch, a pill said to share strangely similar properties to Viagra. "Bandstand" also featured a nerdy Tom Verbrick in horn-rimmed glasses — a role often employed by the troupe. He and other cast members would revisit the character in later Frank productions.

Warren Gerds gave "Bandstand" a perfect four-star review despite stating that some of the comedy fell flat. He did note the increased structure in the performance, but it was the aforementioned commercials and the singing that had the critic most impressed.

Despite the perfect review, the troupe would return to doing more revue-based shows as they had done previously until fall of 2005.

"At one point I think Pat and I asked ourselves how many fucking more revue shows can we possibly do? Are we going to keep impersonating people forever?" recalls Frank.

Previously, the troupe had found a comfortable place doing revue shows, which were made up of bits, skits and impersonations and loosely tied together by a genre or decade. A show might center around Broadway musical selections, the music of the 1970s or music from the British invasion of the 1960s and feature impersonations of popular acts for that time period or genre.

The troupe had toyed with a story-lined show with "Bandstand," but with "Beach Baby" they may have perfected it. The storyline followed two female friends (played by Shelly Lahti-Emmer and Jenny Thiel) from Hortonville who win a trip to California. Complete with a collection of '60s and '70s hits and a Beach Boys ensemble, the show was a hit.

The show received a perfect, four-star review by Warren Gerds, who made mention that a full house of "people were gasping for air" over the comedy duo of Frank Hermans and Pat Hibbard. Frank sported a gold lamé speedo (and little else) for much of the performance.

Frank's was still moving forward. With "Beach Baby" the troupe had hit on a formula that would serve as the framework for future shows and people were taking notice. New faces were appearing in the crowd ready to discover the troupe and falling in love with their original material.

"All of a sudden we started seeing new people at the shows," recalls Frank. "Bus tours began to show up and new faces began to appear along with the regulars in the crowd."

The days of cranking out a revue show in a single night over a handful of napkins was over. Admittedly, writing shows that divided the balance between the music and the story equally required more work and more time, but the rewards were worth the effort.

To develop their story ideas, Frank and Pat would often rent a room at the Radisson for a weekend where they'd brainstorm ideas for the next show, keeping distractions at arms' length.

"We'd put a white piece of paper on the wall and spitball ideas and write stuff down and then look at it the next morning and say, 'What the hell is that?'" says Hibbard.

With the new formula bringing new faces into the crowd, any lingering doubts Frank might have had about the success of his troupe were put to rest. Performing didn't have to be a hobby, just a thing done in between time spent at one's "real" job, and given where things were with his partners, maybe it shouldn't be.

Just as things were reaching their highest point and the troupe was enjoying its greatest success to date, things behind the scenes were starting to unravel. And as the saying goes: When it rains, it pours. For Frank this was true and obstacles would need to be faced on multiple fronts.

Still working as a salaried employee for Sports Corner and SC Grand, and armed not only with an intimate knowledge of the business and bar operations, but also an intimate knowledge of the revenue generated by Frank's Dinner Theatre, Frank began noticing that not all was adding up around him. Things within the business weren't striking him as copacetic and, as far as he could tell, inconsistencies began showing up on the books. Simply put: By Frank's assessment, the money being taken in, simply wasn't relative to the money being doled out.

His suspicions were heightened when a "math genius" friend took a look at Frank's books and found discrepancies.

Naturally, Frank approached his partners about the discrepancies, but didn't get very far. He was told the percentage in question represented what the business had pulled out to cover the troupe's prop expenses. A fair answer had Frank not budgeted and paid for the troupe's props himself. In Frank's opinion thing's still didn't add up, but making no headway there was little he could do.

Behind the stage things weren't much better and the troupe's afore mentioned bacchanal ways were beginning to take a toll. After exhausting all other options, Darren Johnson and Frank parted ways. Described by both Frank and Pat as an amazing performer and perhaps the most innately talented member of the troupe, Darren — who had been there since "The Temp" days — was there no more.

"It was like losing a brother," says Frank. "He is an amazing performer — amazing, but when you're in a group like this, it isn't just about hurting yourself; if you aren't doing your part, you're letting everyone down."

Frank has called the decision possibly the most difficult he has ever made. To date, Darren and Frank do not speak. The former declined requests to be interviewed for this book.

Like any bad breakup, it's generally best if you don't see your ex for a while, but just because Darren was no longer in the troupe, didn't mean having him out of the picture entirely; instead Frank's partners let Darren return to the Sports Corner and start doing his own shows.

This marked uncertain times for Frank and the troupe.

With his partners' untidy business practices and Darren still performing under a roof that Frank co-owned, something had to give.

— A Message from Frank —

Our first really scripted story format shows were "Bandstand" and "Beach Baby" that Pat and I wrote. Legit theatre? No way! We had blocking assignments, choreography and full dialogue along with great music ... a real show. You know what? We were pros and it was so easy to write, I mean the ideas did not stop coming. Pat and I could have written five shows out of that one show. This made us think that this was the direction to head in and made us wonder why we hadn't done this before? How many different '50s, '60s and '70s revues can you do? Warren Gerds agreed and gave us a four star rating for the show and it was the best selling show (besides Christmas) for many years. We had struck gold. We have since performed the show in three different runs. Look for it again in 2019 for our 20-year anniversary. The gold lame speedo scene in that show has become legendary — folklore in the Let Me Be Frank community.

Being that we were now doing truly scripted shows meant learning your stuff and not just winging it on stage as many were accustomed to doing … mostly me. Dialogue had to be learned to set up the joke, movement had to be remembered to get to the point you wanted to make. This was not so new to us as we all had theatre backgrounds and had performed in many shows. And our performers all were getting paid and paid well, this was the big leagues. I referred back to my time at summer theatre at St. Norbert with the Birders and kind of followed suit. This show was a catalyst for the remainder of the LMBF's shows, and it proved we could make a living doing this stuff!

I hope someday I am able to mend my relationship with Darren. Many hurtful things have been said over the years, things I wish I could take back. The truth is, I respect the creative genius and performing genius of this man. I wish him and his troupe only the best and continued success. I do miss our time together, my friend.

ACT III

The Key to the City

IVE GOT A GOLDEN TICKET OR
WITHOUT (BARELY) A SCRATCH

Perhaps not evident to audiences, which were turning out in record numbers to see the troupe's shows, but things behind the scenes were changing. When they had started back in '99, all was just a pipe dream, a way to have fun, a way to spend time with friends. By the mid-2000s, Frank was starting to believe that performing was something he — and his crew — could make a living at, but with a deteriorating relationship with his business partners and former Frank's performer Darren Johnson still underfoot, the SC Grand was looking less and less hospitable. Frank secretly began working on an exit strategy.

As Frank begins to feel the proverbial walls closing in upon him and is seeking a way out, a chain of events set in motion years earlier is about to present Frank with a most fortuitous solution.

In 1998, two years after Frank and brother Mike have closed up Doc's Laff Factory, sitting a mere stones throw from where Doc's had been, the once proud life of Green Bay's Fox Theatre is seemingly at an end.

By the late '90s, the theatre, which had opened on Valentine's Day in 1930 and once hosted the likes of Nat King Cole, Roy Rogers and Louis Armstrong, has seen better days. In 1978, the struggling Bay Theatre, as it was then called, was sold to Standard Theatres and converted into a tri-plex movie theatre. Twenty years later, on November 1, 1998, Standard Theatres locked the doors and walked away from the venue. The closure caught the community off guard.

"It just happened out the blue. They literally walked away, shut off the heat and were doing nothing," says Kramer Rock, the Meyer Theatre's first board chairman.

When the historic venue's doors were closed for what appeared the last time on the verge of a Wisconsin winter, he and a group of others that included area builder and businessman Harry Macco and then-mayor Paul Jadin, sprang to action with the purpose of saving the building from the wrecking ball. By 2000 the group had incorporated and a capital campaign to restore the building to its former glory was underway.

To oversee renovations, the group hired architect Mark Faller. Faller and his father had previously restored the Pabst Theatre in Milwaukee and seemed the perfect fit to return the tri-plex to its former self.

With their goal of saving and restoring the venue well in hand, a new task was set before the venue's supporters. Saving the building was one thing, but keeping the doors open, and the light's on, another.

"We were well intentioned, but didn't have two nickels to rub together and no skill set to run a damn theatre," says Rock.

Rock, who was a member of a committee at UWGB responsible for finding the university's next chancellor, used his connections there to land management for the newly remodeled venue. Rock was able to convince the current chancellor that having the Weidner Center manage the Meyer Theatre as another source of income might be a good idea.

On Valentine's Day, 2002, the Meyer Theatre opened its doors to the public with the Weidner Center acting as management. A great task had been accomplished, but there was more work to be done.

The venue was alive and kicking, but the Meyer struggled to meet its financial obligations to the managing Weidner Center. Meanwhile, a waning interest in Broadway shows and the opening of the Fox Cities Performing Arts Center that November left the Weidner Center with problems of its own. According to Rock, by 2003, he sensed the need to seek alternative management for the theatre.

"The only other game in town at the time was PMI," says Rock.

In May of 2004, the Meyer Theatre Board of Directors announced PMI as the venue's new management company.

"What I knew about running PACs you could fit in a thimble," admits Rock.

He and other board members traveled to other performing arts houses in an attempt to better understand how best to keep the Meyer's doors open for years to come. However, unlike theatres in Manitowoc or Sheboygan, the Meyer, which had to compete with the Weidner, Resch and others, would likely be limited to running 60 or 70 performances per year. Fewer shows meant less revenue and presented a challenge to the Meyer's board members.

The key, according to Kramer, was finding a way to keep the Meyer's lights on. One day, while looking out the window, the answer came to him: The Meyer needed a house troupe.

"It was like literally the clichéd light bulb went off," says Rock, "and I'm thinking, 'Who the hell would I know that had a troupe going?'"

Familiar with Frank as the voice of the Radisson and having caught a show or two at the SC Grand, Kramer, without seeking board member approval, called Frank to set up a meeting.

"I tend to do these things independently," says Rock. "That way if it takes a dump; no harm, no foul … it's infinitely easier, as the saying goes, to ask for forgiveness than it is to ask permission."

That initial meeting took place in a seating area on the Meyer's second floor. Nothing was signed that day, but Frank who "didn't know Kramer from Adam," left that meeting with a dizzy head but knowing he had a way to get out of the SC Grand.

"My brain was going a hundred miles an hour when I left that meeting," says Frank. "I was making plans, thinking of how I could do this."

Undoubtedly ready to burst, Frank restrained himself and told no one about his meeting with Kramer.

Up to that point, Frank's head had been on a swivel, looking for venues where he might be able to move his troupe and get a clean start. With this new deal taking shape, Frank's attentions could now be directed at making the break from the Grand as cleanly as possible.

As Frank explains, he couldn't just walk away from all he'd built. His name was now bigger than himself and represented more than the starry eyed kid from Denmark that could sing like Elvis. Frank was now not only a man, but a brand, and a profitable one at that — profitable enough that people were willing to fight over it.

Once all was in order and the move to the Meyer a sure thing, Frank approached his partners at the SC Grand with the news. Frank asked to be bought out of his percentage of the business and would resign from his duties as bar manager and instead focus only on the troupe.

"It was bad. It almost went to fisticuffs numerous times," says Frank. "It was three against one. They couldn't stand me and I couldn't stand them."

Ultimately, there was some confusion as to who owned or had dibs on the unofficial rights of Frank's Dinner Theatre, as the group had never really incorporated. Frank, naturally, saw the troupe as his, the Grand believed it was theirs. Perhaps realizing that without Frank there likely was no troupe, and not wanting to lose the revenue that it generated, a deal was struck.

Frank was relieved from his duties as partner and bar manager, but would continue to head up, not only the troupe, but all the entertainment needs of the Grand for the 2006 season. The Grand, however, would retain the Frank's Dinner Theatre name to use even after he left, or so the plan went. Frank obliged and the his troupe was renamed Let Me Be Frank Productions.

Despite a now obvious rift between Frank and his former partners, the Grand did make one last ditch effort to keep the troupe indefinitely and offered him a deal nearly identical to that being offered by the Meyer. Knowing what he knew, he declined. Let Me Be Frank Productions would be moving to the Meyer ... if they survived the 2006 season.

This transitional period remained a highly bewildering time and while it's difficult to know just how much of this audiences could detect, a look at the 2006 SC Grand Dinner Theatre guide (the precursor to today's PlayFrank) reveals clues to this tumultuous time.

To any serious collector of Frank memorabilia, the 2006 guide is a must-have. If it was a stamp it might not have been a British Guiana 1c Magenta, but it could have been an Inverted Jenny or at the very least a Penny Black. If a baseball card, think Honus Wagner's 1910 Standard Carmel card versus his Sweet Caporal Cigarettes card. If a comic book, it may not be Action Comics No.1, but it could certainly have been Action Comics No. 23.

Inside, Frank introduces the troupe as Let Me Be Frank Productions for the first time, as well as names Pat Hibbard as his new business partner. He introduces Paul Evansen — essentially Darren's replacement — as a full-time member of the troupe and notes the return of founding member Amy Riemer-Kruk from Texas. Even her then-husband, Jason Kruk, appears as one of the troupe's players.

It is also where the move to the Meyer Theatre is announced publically to fans (an official announcement had appeared in the Press-Gazette) — Frank, not one to air the laundry publically, sites a need for a bigger space as the motivation for the move and thanks the SC Grand for a great run. Also in the guide is a desultory announcement that among other things, introduces Darren as executive director and producer of the Grand's house entertainment after the current troupe moves to the Meyer. In it, Darren states the "intimate 232 person Dinner Theatre is where we want to be," even calling the venue "perfect" before wishing Frank and company well. In closing, readers are told to "be comfortable in the fact" that he and the new troupe were there for them.

The Let Me Be Frank schedule for 2006 included a "Best of 2005" show, "Hee Haw Hoe Down," "Frankstock," "Bandstand II," "Hollywood Nights" and "A Frank's Christmas."

2006 also had the troupe performing their first show at the Meyer Theatre. As part of a trial run or testing of the waters, Let Me Be Franks would re-prise 2005's "Drive-in Movie" for a one-week run at the Meyer.

With an end in sight, all Frank would have to do would be to survive the year, but that may not have been as easy as it sounds.

"You see this light at the end of the tunnel and you feel there's no obstacle to get there," says Frank.

Frank was optimistic and perhaps over-simplifying the situation. With the word out that he and the troupe would be moving, his former business part-ners did little to make the troupe's final year at the Grand a smooth one and at times seemed to purposely make things difficult for Frank.

"It was a nightmare," recalls Frank. "Nothing seemed to go smoothly. They fought me on everything."

That year, disputes over the troupe's expenses between Frank and the venue would have both parties in small claims court several times. Paired with the monumental change of moving to the Meyer on the horizon, the adjust-ment to making ends meet financially as the troupe's owner and his former friend and colleague itching to usurp him, things began to take their toll. At home, Frank's marriage was suffering and soon his health would follow. Frank ultimately ended up in the emergency room with chest pains. Doc-tors would reveal that what he had believed was a heart attack was, in fact, a stress induced panic attack.

The walls felt as if they were closing in around him. In such times, a person looks for comfort wherever they can find it. Sometimes that comfort can be found right under our very noses. For Frank, a growing friendship with Amy provided him the comfort he sought.

The two had known each other for years, but there had never been any sparks between them. In fact, Frank claims quite the opposite and insists Amy didn't think very highly of him at all. Amy doesn't seem too quick to refute that thought.

Frank sites one of his infamous wardrobe malfunctions while at the Sports Corner as evidence. Back when all was makeshift, Amy walked in on a naked Frank who sat smoking a cigarette in the men's "dressing room." Unfazed by the incident, Frank gave a wide-eyed Amy his best head nod and a smooth "Hey, how's it going?" Amy wasn't impressed.

Another incident between them that left Amy visibly upset with Frank involved the casting for "Beach Baby." Amy was sidelined for that show and not given a part in the cast.

Until her permanent return to Wisconsin in 2005, Amy had been living in Texas and working as a schoolteacher. During summer breaks, Amy would return to Wisconsin and perform with the troupe during its summer show. Unable to make the trip and participate during the summer of 2004, Frank assumed Amy wouldn't be back in 2005 to participate in "Drive-in Movie."

Remembering how unorganized and last minute things were during her other performances with the troupe, Amy was shocked to find things had changed when she called from Texas to inform Frank of her return to Wisconsin and desire to again participate.

"I was very used to them doing things very fly-by-the-seat-of-your-pants. I hadn't realized, especially having been gone for over a year, that they had actually gotten their crap together and gotten organized," says Amy.

An excited Amy was deflated to hear the parts had already been cast.

"I was like, it's only February, Frank. Really, you know this far in advance?"

Amy would end up in the show, but not as she was accustomed. Keyboardist Tony Pilz, in order to spend time with his family, began taking summer shows off. Frank, perhaps having felt guilty for not having had checked with Amy before casting the show, asked her to cover keyboard duties during the show.

Amy, who is no keyboarder, told Frank she was "Awful! Completely, totally awful."

78

"I told him, 'You do not want me to play keyboards in your show, I'm dead serious.'"

Frank, true to form, didn't listen and persisted, even calling Amy's mother to express how much he wanted her to do the show. In the end, Amy agreed and "worked her ass off" to learn her parts.

The general consensus on Amy's keyboard performance: not bad.

Despite his eagerness to cast Amy in "Drive-in Movie," Frank wasn't so quick to cast her in the troupe's next show, the first run of "Beach Baby." Having scripted the show in advance, and not knowing that Riemer would be returning to Wisconsin, the show's script called for only two female roles — and both had been cast already.

The snub has turned into a comedic anecdote in the couple's history as Amy will, from time to time, remind Frank that he needn't feel bad when he must disappoint a cast member by telling them no … as he seemingly had no problem telling her no when casting "Beach Baby."

Ultimately, the two connected upon their similarities, each lending the other a shoulder to lean on. Both had children with autism and both were weathering rocky marriages, but the two remained friends … for now, anyways.

— A Message from Frank —

In the year 2006, my health declined and I needed to do something about it. I had been a closet smoker and needed to quit, I had used recreational drugs and I needed to quit, I drank every show and needed to quit. I had gained over twenty-five pounds due to stress and my knees were giving out and needed to be replaced. I was in deep shit; I needed a life change and some hard kicks to the head to get on track. I had a panic attack one day at the SC Grand, Tom Verbrick, who was our bus tour sales dude, drove me to the hospital that day. Tests were run, and I had a cauterization procedure done. They told me something was wrong with me but it wasn't my heart. I was put on some medication that I don't remember at this time to help with anxiety, it just made it worse, and it was the only show I have ever missed in my seventeen years of performing with LMBF. It all changed the day I stepped on the Meyer stage. All of a sudden, I was free. Free to run a business without complications, no more fighting and bickering. I knew a couple things; I knew how to write and produce a show and I knew I had the best cast I could hope for and a partner who had the same vision. And I didn't know at the time … but I had met someone who would change my life forever, Amy Riemer.

FENG SHUI THE GRAND CANYON OR
HIT THE GROUND RUNNING

As should come as no surprise, Frank and company did survive that final year at the Grand. Despite so much going on behind the scenes, the 2006 season was a success at least as far as audiences and critic Warren Gerds were concerned.

The troupe had hit their stride at the most opportune time. They were stepping up to Green Bay's big time … and a very big venue.

Frank and company's trial show at the Meyer had been a success during their brief run in June of '06, but one thing was clear, the Meyer was a large house. The troupe was eager to begin its first full season as the Meyer's house troupe, but before they could, they'd need to rethink some things. The troupe would have to think big.

Obviously, the increased seating capacity of the Meyer presented a great opportunity for the troupe, but the stage itself was considerably larger than the cabaret stage they had utilized at the Grand.

A typical Frank show calls for a cast of six performers and a four-piece band, but when upon the Meyer's 52-foot wide, 22-foot tall, presidium stage, the cast ended up looking more like dwarves about to crush an 18-inch foam Stonehenge monument than a legit musical-comedy troupe.

"That was it. The first thing I had to figure out was how to make us look legit on that massive stage. Once you get on stage, it doesn't seem so big, but when you're in the audiences looking at the stage, that's when things seem really big. "

The first part of Frank's solution was to add a backdrop. Frank had always hoped to utilize backdrops in the troupe's shows, but the absence of a fly loft upon the SC Grand stage made utilizing a backdrop problematic. The Meyer's fly loft presented Frank with the opportunity.

A search led him to Grosh Backdrop and Drapery, a professional stage company located on West Sunset Blvd in Los Angeles. Since 2007, they've created the backdrops utilized by the troupe during Meyer performances and Frank budgets $2,000 for the creation of each new backdrop.

Another measure to increase the stage presence of the troupe involved the creation of a new, larger riser for the band. The task was turned over to Tim Funk who created a 2-foot tall, riser comprised of six interchangeable 4-foot by 8-foot sections. The new riser not only elevated the band, but allowed the riser to be configured differently for different shows. Tim was also responsible for the creation of many of the troupe's props, which are often reused — sometimes with a fresh coat of paint — for multiple shows. Soon after the troupe moved to the Meyer, Tim Funk, who'd been a part-time sound and stage worker for the troupe since its earliest days, was hired to be the Meyer's technical director — a fulltime position he holds to this day. With years of working together, and an intimate familiarity of how the troupe preferred its lighting and sound duties handled, having Tim Funk at the larger and more professionally equipped Meyer eased the troupe's transitional woes considerably.

On the business side of things, Frank had learned much from his business endeavor with the Sports Corner and SC Grand. Those enterprises were split in such a way that Van Den Heuvel Electric owned 50 percent of the business while he and his three partners collectively owned the other half. Never again would Frank make the mistake of entering into a business venture holding a minority share. Whether that meant owning 51 percent or 75 percent, Frank has insisted on majority ownership of all his business dealings since, including Let Me Be Frank Productions, Frank's Tribute and Frankly Green Bay.

Despite a feeling like he needed to be in charge, another obstacle would present itself at the Meyer Theatre. While only a minority owner of the Sports Corner and Grand, Frank was used to being in charge, at least relatively speaking. He ran the show (and more) at the Grand and wasn't accustomed to sharing creative control with others or having to go through channels to get things done. But where the SC Grand, from a certain point of view, could be seen as *his*, the Meyer Theatre was not. And Frank had to learn to play nice with others.

When PMI agreed to manage the Meyer Theatre in 2004, Matt Goebel, who had been active as the general manager for the Green Bay Blizzard was hired to serve in that capacity for the Meyer Theatre. Frank, accustomed to doing things under a system of autonomy, found his ideas occasionally at odds with Matt's.

In some ways, Frank's move to the Meyer meant he was relieved of at least some of the burdens he had been responsible for in the past. It was no longer solely Frank's responsibility to market the troupe and worry about getting people through the door. He now had Matt to take on those concerns, but Frank, always the promoter, wasn't quick to share the burden.

"In the beginning, there were obviously some challenges," says Goebel. "He was used to doing things his way and we were used to doing things our way, so it was all about finding a way to make those things work for both of us to be successful."

Early in their relationship, Frank felt as though he was being circumvented in areas of discussion, claiming Goebel was likely more willing to approach the easier-going Pat Hibbard with information than himself.

Goebel, who was relatively unfamiliar with the group, did not understand the dynamic that existed within, and insists he was just doing his best to forge a good relationship with all of Frank's members.

Pat has admitted that when it comes to the management and promotional side of the troupe, he could take it or leave it, stating that Frank is "super comfortable doing all that and I'm super comfortable having him do it." How many of the important decisions that Matt and Pat discussed made their way back to Frank is anyone's guess. But, all parties say that communication between them is greatly improved. Now, 10 years on, the differing styles of Matt and Frank appear more an asset than a hindrance. And any differences the two may have had in those early days pale in comparison to the repeated near fisticuff "conferences" that Frank had with his former partners. And although it was ultimately Matt's concern to encourage audiences through the Meyer doors, the contract that PMI and LMBF's had agreed upon would still require Frank's promotional prowess. And both men would be called upon to put their marketing skills to the test if Let Me Be Franks was to be a long-term success at the Meyer.

It may be difficult to imagine that The Frankman has ever had a problem with branding, but that simply isn't the case. In fact, Frank's branding of the dinner theatre may have been too good as when he and the majority of the cast left for the Meyer and effectively left the SC Grand holding onto the Frank's Dinner Theatre title, many fans couldn't grasp the changes as they unfolded. Despite announcements in the Grand's playbill the previous year and coverage in the Press-Gazette announcing the troupe's move, many fans simply didn't latch onto the idea that Frank's troupe was now Let Me Be Franks and had moved downtown.

Many a confused fan found themselves attending a Frank's Dinner Theatre show in 2007 or '08 that didn't include Frank and the majority of the cast to which they'd grown accustomed. To address the confusion, PMI's vice president of marketing and communications, Kathie Mickle, came up with an aggressive "Where's Frank?" print campaign that ran in the Press-Gazette.

The campaign was generally successful, but not entirely.

"To this day, people still call us Frank's Dinner Theatre," says Frank. "If you didn't live in Green Bay and didn't get the Press-Gazette, you didn't know that we'd moved. It was hard to get people to understand we'd moved."

But move they had. Let Me Be Frank's would kick off their first full season at the Meyer Theatre by offering five original shows, "Frank's Country Jamboree," "Me & Bobby McGee," "Rock Around the Clock," "Viva Las Vegas" and "A Frank's Christmas."

In March or 2007, Frank and company took the stage for their first official performance as the Meyer's house troupe. Their first offering: "Frank's Country Jamboree."

The show poked fun at Frank's farm boy roots. Its story, set in fictional Toad Lick County, had the F.F.A.A. guys (that's Future Farmers Anonymous of America) square off against the girls from 5-H (as opposed to 4-H) to present judges at the county fair with the most inventive use of manure.

Generally free of butterflies during a Let Me Be Frank performance, the opposite was true for Frank during Elvis impersonator contests. There's something about knowing he's being judged during a competition that sets his nerves on edge. And during this initial show at the Meyer, it was fair to say he and the troupe were indeed being judged. Frank was nervous.

"To be honest, I was shitting bricks that first night up on stage," admits Frank.

It wasn't until he sang his first song that the adrenalin and the applause of the crowd carried him the rest of the way. The judges had approved.

Warren Gerds awarded the show a perfect four-stars. In his review he wrote that the troupe had "come out roaring" in its first "official" Meyer performance, but that didn't mean all was perfect.

Gerds mentioned the group's ballads were "too few" and described the sound as "too hot" for the Meyer's space, but those concerns were drops in the bucket. The troupe would have many opportunities ahead of them in which to adjust to their new surroundings and change things up.

Many concerned individuals had been pulling for Frank and his troupe, hoping that they were the right fit to revitalize a long-neglected corner of downtown Green Bay and keep the Meyer's future bright.

Perhaps no one in Green Bay has been so closely linked to the revitalization of the city's downtown than Jeff Mirkes. As the executive director of Downtown Green Bay, Inc. and Olde Main Street, Inc., as well as the board president of the Meyer Theatre, Jeff's interest in a thriving downtown cannot be overstated, nor can the Meyer's connection to that revitalization.

"The Meyer Theatre is extremely integral to downtown's success," says Mirkes. "Frank's intangible impact on the Meyer goes far beyond the number of tickets sold."

Frank's troupe could do more than just leave the lights on; it could help keep the Meyer, an anchor point of Green Bay's resurging downtown, a fixture all year round.

"There's a lot of things that Let Me Be Franks does for the theatre that cannot be accomplished in other ways," says Goebel. "Typically, theatres of this size around the country, they pretty much go dark in the summer. Frank's summer shows keep the building occupied and it keeps it busy with traffic coming through."

Gerds may have said it best in that initial review for "Frank's Country Jamboree."

He wrote, "Where else have you heard of a local outfit being gutsy enough — and good enough — to take on a long-term gig in a downtown theater? Not anyplace near Green Bay, for sure."

— *A Message from Andrew* —

Into each life some rain …

What you hold in your hands today isn't to be misconstrued as a tell-all book; it is not. Originally, Frank had hoped to simply tell the story of how Let Me Be Frank Productions and its offshoots came to be. What he failed to realize is that to tell that story requires that Frank be in it. This posed a few problems moving ahead.

It may come as a surprise to some, including his fans, but for a man that is so readily at home in front of an audience or camera, Frank is a relatively private person. When sitting down to our first of many meetings to create this book, it became apparent that Frank's private side was tucked safely away.

Perhaps the most difficult of tasks concerning this book was to convince Frank to open up to some vulnerability. But to know Frank, at least as he is today, is to know that he is not one to fan the flames of gossip. He is not quick to criticize others or make comparisons. He has during his lifetime been hurt, presumably, quite deeply. And this author has found his aversion to hurt others, even where potentially justified to do so, edifying. Instead, he is quick to forgive — some would even say that he forgives too quickly. But he is, it seems, acutely aware of his potential to hurt others. And it is for this reason, and that he is co-author of this project, that many of the rainy aspects of his life have been omitted from the text.

Let it suffice to say that they haven't all been good days for Frank. His parents divorced when he was young, he's had two marriages fail, he's had to sit in court against business partners he once called friends and even had members of his own troupe plot against him, but these are not aspects of his life that he wished to explore within these pages.

These things are mentioned only to exhibit that there have been other obstacles along the way, and to acknowledge that this book's authors are aware that such details are missing — that's by design.

Having said that, our story is far from over.

Frank, in many ways, is larger than life. His name has taken on many meanings, both to his fans and himself.

"I know," says Frank, "that when someone asks, 'How's Frank?' they don't mean me, they mean Let Me Be Franks, or Frank's Tribute or Frankly Green Bay or any of the other things I'm a part of."

There's much more to Frank than we've discussed here. Champion for local charities, news anchor, telethon host, publisher, husband, father, Elvis impersonator and even hero, we've only scratched the surface as to who Frank is, but those are stories for another time.

To be continued …

LET ME BE FRANK TRIVIA

1. Which Let Me Be Frank performer struggles with bowed vocal cords?

2. In what country outside the U.S. did Frank perform as Elvis in 2010?

3. Which current Let Me Be Frank cast member was discovered by Frank at UWGB while scouting Emily Paulsen?

4. Which current cast member is obsessed with Disney?

5. Which current LMBF's cast member is deaf in one ear?

6. How many years has LMBF's been the main entertainment during the CP telethon?

7. Which LMBF's cast member was a teacher in Texas?

8. Which current Let Me Be Frank cast member was a stunt double for Jay Leno?

9. What popular Wisconsin band was Dennis Panneck in during the 1990s?

10. What did Frank originally want to name the troupe?

11. Which of the following is not one of Frank's bands?
    A. Section 8
    B. The Hard Ways
    C. The Rude Boys
    D. Facked

12. What is your name? What is your quest? What is your favorite color?

ANSWERS

1. Pat Hibbard
Pat has bowed vocal cords and his left vocal cord was partially paralyzed after the extensive radiation treatment he received as a teen. At times, he finds it even difficult to speak.

2. Israel
Frank visited the country as part of cultural exchange grant between UWGB and Tel-Aviv University.

3. Lisa Borley
Lisa was discovered by Emily during a UWGB performance of 'Urine-town.'

4. Kasey Corrado
Kasey plans vacations to the magical kingdom regularly.

5. Amy Riemer

6. 12
2016 will mark the 12th time LMBF's has been involved with the CP telethon.

7. Amy Riemer
While she participated in early Frank's Dinner Theatre shows, Amy moved to Texas where she was a school music teacher. She returned regularly every summer to participate in a Frank's show until 2005 when she returned permanently.

8. Tom Verbrick
Tom was called upon to act as Jay Leno's stunt double in a bit that had Leno shagging fly balls from MLB slugger Frank Thomas.

9. Juke Box Heroes

10. The Nicolet Players

11. B. The Hard Ways

12. How should we know?

ABOUT THE AUTHORS

Frank Hermans is a musician and entertainer living in Brillion, Wis. He founded Let Me Be Frank Productions with Pat Hibbard in 2005 and has won multiple Best of the Bay awards as voted by the readers of the Green Bay Press-Gazette. Frank is a fill-in news anchor and co-host for WFRV-TV 5 and his Frankly Green Bay television segment airs every Wednesday a.m. on that channel.

Andrew Kruse-Ross is a writer and editor living in Green Bay, Wis. He is the former editor of Scene Newspaper and The Chilton Times-Journal. In 2015, he co-founded the monthly arts and entertainment publication Frankly Green Bay with Frank and Mike Hermans. He is a graduate of the University of Michigan-Flint.